A Year on the Fosse

The Wildlife and History of the famous Roman Road

A journey through the year from Lincolnshire to Devon

'They are the most ignorant people I have ever conquered.'
(Julius Caesar, writing home about the Britons)

'Do not buy slaves in England.
They cannot be taught to read and are the
ugliest and most stupid race I ever saw.'
(Cicero writing to his friend Atticus)

Peregrine

Rick Thompson

Grosvenor House
Publishing Limited

This book is published by
Grosvenor House Publishing Ltd
Link House
140 The Broadway, Tolworth, Surrey, KT6 7HT.
www.grosvenorhousepublishing.co.uk

A CIP record for this book
is available from the British Library

ISBN 978-1-80381-199-4

Contents

Preface

Workmen digging the foundations for new buildings in the grounds of Warwick School in 2018 made a surprising discovery. The excavators fell silent and the archeologists were called in. They had uncovered the stone remains of a large structure, described as the size of a medieval church. It had suites of rooms with a central isle, and corn-drying ovens. What was so surprising was that this was no medieval building. It was Roman.

Until then, the county town of Warwickshire in the centre of England had revealed little evidence of Roman occupation. Its origins are known to be Saxon. The town was founded in the year 914 when Alfred the Great's daughter, Aethelflaed, built a wooden fortress on a rocky bluff on the north bank of the Warwickshire Avon, as a defence against marauding Danes. Indeed she is said to have founded the original Warwick School in the castle, making it one of the oldest schools in the country. There are plenty of Roman artefacts and coin-hoards in the county museum collection, but none of them was found in Warwick itself.

The foundations unearthed on the south bide of the Warwickshire Avon showed that the building had been expanded twice over a couple of hundred years, with the final stone structure 18 metres long, with glass windows and a cluster of outbuildings. But what was it? Not a farm. Certainly not a grand house or villa, because there were no domestic artefacts. Dr. Jerry Evans of Archeology Warwickshire told me, "It would have been the largest building in the whole of the Midlands, but it is a conundrum." Principal Archeologist Stuart Palmer said, "The building probably forms a component of a large villa estate, which must have spread along the banks of the Avon and been connected to the Roman road system." So it was probably involved in the construction or maintenance of one of the earliest, longest and straightest Roman Roads in England running past just 3 miles away – the Fosse Way.

Warwick is my home town. It lies close to the central section of the great Fosse Way linking Exeter and Lincoln. I've driven along sections of the Roman road many times, wondering how it was built, and how its existence has shaped much of central England, with towns that sprang up at crossroads and river-crossings along its length flourishing to this day. Some have names that proudly proclaim their origins more than two thousand years ago: Stretton-under-Fosse, Fossebridge, Lydford-on-Fosse and so on. This straight line is like a slice cut through the heart of England, revealing our origins.

Along its 230-mile length there are many different natural habitats, from the flat arable lands of Lincolnshire and the rolling East Midland Wolds, through the Heart of England Forest, The Cotswolds Area of Outstanding Natural Beauty, the sumptuous cider country of Somerset and Devon, to the muddy estuaries of Axmouth and Exmouth. I decided to explore the Fosse Way on visits through the year, discovering the stories of the cities, towns and villages along its route, and observing the wildlife to be found in reserves, parks and the open countryside as the seasons changed.

I live as far from the sea as it is possible to do in England, and still have a childlike thrill when approaching a coastal resort, smelling the salt in the air, and then glimpsing the glittering ocean ahead. So I decided to make my journey towards the sea, travelling south-west from Lincoln in January to the Devon coast in December. I found many intriguing stories, fascinating wildlife, and some extremely attractive places, rich in history. I hope you enjoy joining me on this journey through the heart of England, in the footsteps of the extraordinary Romans who built The Fosse Way.

THE
FOSSE
WAY

LINCOLN

NEWARK

NOTTINGHAM ○

LEICESTER ○

COVENTRY ○
LEAMINGTON SPA ○

MORETON-IN-MARSH

STOW-ON-THE-WOLD

CIRENCESTER

BATH

CHIPPENHAM

SHEPTON MALLET

ILCHESTER

EXETER

AXMINSTER

EXMOUTH

N
W · E
S

Introduction

Caesar and his Men

Veni, Vidi, Vici. (I came; I saw; I conquered).
(Julius Caesar)

Kestrel

Invasion

At my grammar school, I had to study Latin. I found it a struggle. But I wanted to go to university to study English, and for that course most higher education establishments required Latin O-Level. So I had to buckle down and learn my *amo, amas, amat,* which means I love, you love, and he/she/it loves. I certainly didn't love Latin, and just scraped through the exam at the second attempt.

The set-book for translation was 'Caesar's Gallic Wars, Books IV and V'. These accounts are Julius Caesar's diaries of his conquest of large parts of northern Europe, then called Gaul. Books four and five recount his invasions of Britain. We were taught a simple rhyme to remind us of the dates.

> BC 55, Caesar and his men arrive.
> BC 54, Caesar and his men once more.

Trying to translate the original texts was an ordeal, but reading the English translations was much more exciting, with detailed accounts of bloody battles between the Roman invaders and the doughty Celts. The first crossing of the Channel by Caesar's legions in 55 BC was a scoping expedition to a land regarded by the Roman Empire as 'mysterious' but 'well-endowed'. Before the Romans invaded, the British Isles had no single political or cultural identity. It was populated by independent tribal groups, led by powerful kings and queens. The tribes each controlled their own territories and resources, and they didn't always live in peace with one another. But when the powerful Roman armies arrived on their shores, the Celtic tribes in the south of England united against them.

And the invaders were certainly immensely powerful. According to Caesar's diaries, after the scouting expedition in

2

55 BC, he arrived in the following year with 800 ships carrying five well-trained legions and no fewer than 2,000 cavalry with their horses. It must have been an intimidating sight for the Celtic tribesman, who had lined up along the clifftops. In a series of battles, Caesar forged northward, crossing the Thames, and forcing the locals to give him 'tribute' and hostages who would be slain if they failed to pay up. But there was trouble back in mainland Europe, with Gallic tribes waging guerrilla war against the occupiers, so Caesar withdrew his armies from Britain to put down the insurrections. The full scale suppression of the islands of Britain would have to wait until another day. That day was not to come until ninety years later when the Emperor Claudius ordered the full scale invasion of Britain.

Plautius

In AD 43, General Aulus Plautius led a massive invasion force across The Channel. Historians reckon there were probably 40,000 men including four elite legions and auxiliary troops with cavalry. The organisation required to transport such a large force of men, animals and supplies was immense. It probably needed a fleet of as many as 1,000 transport ships and warships for the task.

The Roman army was a formidable machine. The Britons were no match for the well-equipped professional troops, and within a couple of years the Romans had control of the whole of south-east England. But northern tribes and the Welsh to the west continued to launch attacks on the invaders, so Plautius ordered his troops, and no doubt a huge number of locals forced into service, to dig a defensive ditch – a 'fossa' in Latin – all the way from Exeter to Lincoln to protect their territory. It had garrisoned forts at intervals, mainly where it intersected with existing roads such as Ermin Way at Cirencester, and Watling Street heading to North Wales from Dover, and alongside the ditch they constructed a paved road so that troops including chariots could be deployed swiftly to respond to any trouble, and wagons with supplies could be moved in all weathers.

The Agger

So the Fosse Way was one of the very first Roman Roads in Britain, completed just a few years after the massed legions had fought their way ashore. And the road could put our modern potholed efforts to shame. It was beautifully paved. The few remaining sections, such as one near Ilchester, may look like very rough cobbles, but originally the gaps were filled with a kind of concrete, called *opus signinium,* to make a smooth surface suitable for galloping horses and marching men. The road surface is called the 'agger'. It was carefully engineered, with layers of gravel, small stones, then cambered larger slabs, and drainage channels on either side.

It must have been useful that the route matched the geology of central England. The Fosse Way follows the line of the Jurassic band of rocks, with older Triassic to the north-west and more recent Cretaceous to the south-east. In places it follows a limestone ridge, which provided much of the paving for the agger. Many of the Roman quarrying sites turned into pools that to this day are the basis of a chain of nature reserves along the route of the old road. And the Fosse Way was built straight - almost the defining quality of a Roman Road in Britain. Central England doesn't have mountainous barriers and the road-builders didn't need to respect properties or farms. So the Fosse Way deviates from a ruler-straight line by only 6 miles at its bendiest.

Modern Roads

The way passes through eight of the great counties of central England. But of course in Roman times the counties didn't exist. After the withdrawal of the legions in the 5th century, and the period of the regional kingdoms of the Anglo-Saxons, it was the Norman invaders who carved up England into shires. Their Earls exercised control on behalf of the crown through chosen representatives – Sheriffs, Lord Lieutenants, and Justices of the Peace - for the collection of taxes and keeping discipline. But the names of the shires, based on the main market town in the area, often retained elements of their Roman titles. So Leicestershire, (in the Domesday Book of 1068, 'Ledecestre', meaning the people of the River Ligor, now the Soar), is joined with 'ceaster', from the Latin for camp, fort or town. And Gloucestershire couples the Celtic 'Glevo', meaning a bright or pleasant place, with 'ceaster'. The counties morphed into administrative areas of local government as recently as 1889.

Many sections of the Fosse Way form parts of our modern road systems, and in several places the old road defines parish or county boundaries. From Lincoln the A46 follows the route through Leicester, then it's the B4114 and B4455 through Warwickshire, where it joins the A429 all the way to Cirencester. Then its route is followed by the A433, the A367, the A37, and the A303, before wiggling its way through Bath and on to Exeter and the coast.

Some parts of the Roman Fosse Way have been by-passed, and a few sections are country lanes only accessible these days on foot. But the modern roads are pretty close to the original straight line, and there are plenty of opportunities to stop at towns with Roman origins all along the route, and to explore the nature reserves that are dotted along it, some based on ancient quarries.

Greenspace

When the Romans were building the Fosse Way, Britain was a very different place from the one we know. It's estimated that the population was less than 3 million. England was extensively wooded, and most people lived off the land. They must have been completely connected to the natural world, and attuned to the changing seasons. Today the UK population is approaching 70 million with the majority living in large towns and cities, detached from the natural environment. There is little doubt that modern urban living is stressful. Even in the sixteenth century, Shakespeare often contrasted the corruption, violence and scheming of London, and in particular The Court, with the pastoral innocence of the Forest of Arden.

Today, the reserves, parks and other protected natural places along the Fosse Way are particularly valuable resources because they are close to population centres and easy to reach, and because regular contact with nature improves our sense of well-being. Countless studies in Europe, the USA and Japan have been able to measure this. Scientists call it 'exposure to greenspace'. A recent article in New Scientist magazine stated that, 'A growing number of psychologists and ecologists are studying the effects of nature on people's mental health and well-being ... the evidence of positive effects from nature includes therapy for specific psychological conditions such as depression, anxiety and mood disorder. Access to nature has also been found to improve sleep and reduce stress, increase happiness and reduce negative emotions.'

I think this has become particularly important in Britain in recent years when various factors have seen the number people with mental health problems soaring, and NHS services overwhelmed. The 'mental health crisis' achieved wide recognition during the Covid-19 pandemic, when millions suffered financial stress, isolation and separation from loved ones, and it continued with the cost of living crisis. A poll by Mental Health UK at the end of 2022 revealed that financial worries made 10% of us feel 'hopeless', 29% were 'stressed', and 34% were 'living with anxiety'. I feel particularly sorry for children and young people who have had to study from home because of coronavirus or crumbling school buildings, and those who want to move on to higher education know they will start adult life heavily in debt. Surveys show many do not expect to have a better quality of life than their parents. They are said to be the first recorded generation to feel so negative about their prospects. In 2024, the 'World Happiness Report', a barometer of wellbeing in 140 countries coordinated by Oxford University, showed 'disconcerting' drops in youth happiness, especially in North America and Europe. It is clear that contact with the natural environment is becoming increasingly important. Young people also put Climate Change near the top of their worries about the future. They value the natural world and want to protect it.

It seems that contact with nature also helps your physical health as well as your mental state. The doctor and respected writer, broadcaster and podcaster, Dr. Michael Mosley, who died while on holiday on a Greek island in 2024, had addressed this on his BBC Radio series, 'Just One Thing'. In an episode called 'Green Spaces', he said, "Research has shown clearly that being outside in nature can reduce stress, and also that it can benefit your heart and immune system. And the benefits of spending more time in natural settings can have a lasting effect." Clearly it is extremely important to protect our accessible green spaces and stop the decline in biodiversity, for a happier and healthier lifestyle.

I hope the following chapters will encourage you to explore the fascinating towns and attractive villages that grew up along the ancient road, discover some curious stories, but also to take some time out to visit some of the nature reserves, large parks, woods and waterways, and note the uplifting wildlife to be found throughout the year along the course of the Fosse Way.

January

Lincoln to Newark

The pessimist complains about the wind;
the optimist expects it to change;
the realist adjusts the sails
(Dolly Parton)

Cranes

Lindum Colonia – Roman Lincoln

The most striking, and the most photographed reminder of Lincoln's Roman origins is the Newport Arch, once the main north gate of the upper city, carrying Ermine Street from London on towards York. The large limestone slabs of the arch were once connected to defensive towers and a wall that encircled the town. It is said to be the oldest arch in Britain still used by traffic. And in modern times it has had a few brushes with heavy goods vehicles, notably in 1964 when a large Leyland lorry smashed into the top of the arch, nearly bringing the whole lot down. The stonework was carefully repaired, but in 2017 a truck from a local company called Rase Distribution nearly razed it to the ground when it became wedged fast under the arch. The driver told the local press he was just following his sat-nav! After the tyres had been let down, the lorry was able to reverse out, leaving just a few scrapes on the famous arch.

Lincoln is built on a hill, dominating the surrounding flat countryside - an obvious defensive positions for the Romans, who knew it as *Lindum Colonia*. Lincoln Castle on the hilltop is a Norman fortress, but the original fort there was Roman, constructed in about AD 60 to house the Ninth Legion under the reign of Emperor Nero. Down the aptly named Steep Hill, an attractive cobbled road leading south from the hilltop, we find the end of the Fosse Way, and Brayford Pool, with pleasure boats and swans. This is where the River Witham meets The Fossdyke, regarded as the oldest navigable canal in the country, cut by the Romans in about AD 120 to connect Lincoln with the River Trent that leads to the Humber Estuary and the North Sea trading routes.

It may be a bit windy and chilly this January, but the city of Lincoln is a great place to visit at any time of the year. It is steeped in the past. You can take a tour of the Roman remains, starting in the lower town on Fosse Way, where a section of the original road can be viewed from underneath St. Mary's Guildhall. In the park by the council offices, you can see chunks of the Lower West Gate with information boards about the Romans in Lincoln, and the upper East Gate and 'Mint Wall' have preserved sections of the remains from 2,000 years ago. The Upper South Gate foundations are proudly displayed behind a glass panel in a shop at number 44 Steep Hill. At time of writing, it is a nail salon, which might seem to be a very 21st century service, but in fact Roman women enjoyed a manicure, and had their nails coloured and shaped to show that they didn't need to do any manual work. It seems from statues and murals that they favoured medium length rounded nails.

The South Gate was a monumental structure, with a broad flight of steps leading up to crenellated towers and a double arch. At the top of Steep Hill you can see cobbled roundels on the pavements. These were the bases of rows of columns. It doesn't take much imagination to envisage the magnificent colonnade that would have greeted merchants arriving along the Fosse Way or Ermin Street, impressing on them that *Lindum Colonia* was one of the most important Roman cities in Britain.

The nearby Museum of Lincolnshire Life celebrates the rural and industrial past of the city, and just behind is a beautifully restored windmill with white cap and sails. Ellis Mill dates from the 18th century, and was one of nine windmills on Lincoln hilltop. It's still in working order and on open days you can buy freshly milled flour there. Lincoln tends to be a bit of a windy city, but these days the mid-winter winds are generally quite mild. As the climate changes, the bitter cold days and blizzards of my childhood are becoming a distant memory. The temperature this January is well above freezing with streaks of purple clouds moving from west to east against the pale yellow sky. It's been a wet winter so far. Serious floods have affected much of central England and Wales at the turn of the year, with the Environment Agency overwhelmed in places, and thousands of properties flooded. Lincoln on its rocky outcrop has been unaffected.

The Cathedral

Lincoln Cathedral beside the castle is huge and magnificent. John Ruskin liked it: "I have always held that the Cathedral of Lincoln is out and out the most precious piece of architecture in the British Isles and roughly speaking worth any two other cathedrals we have." Not a bad review. When a five-hundred-foot central spire was completed in 1311, Lincoln Cathedral became the tallest building in the world - the first structure to hold that title since the Great Pyramid of Giza. Unfortunately Lincoln lost its title in 1548 when the spire collapsed in a storm.

Peregrines have been nesting in the cathedral's central tower for a few years now. These gorgeous falcons - the fastest creatures on Earth reaching 200 mph in a dive - certainly keep the number of pigeons down, and with their dashing flight and squeaky calls, they provide some great entertainment over the centre of the city. In January the falcons are already preparing to mate and nest. In 2023 the resident female, known locally as 'Queen', who had successfully reared young in the tower for several years, was seen to dive into some trees and possibly clipped a branch because she didn't reappear. Prime nest sites are at a premium for the expanding number of peregrines; nearly every cathedral has a resident pair. So within days there were two young females making themselves known to the resident male. He chose one who saw off her rival, and the Lincoln peregrines will continue to rear young and entertain us with their aerobatics.

Cranes

And looking up, there's always the chance of seeing some even rarer birds high above, like a group of thin crosses against the pale winter sky as they head for their roosts in reed beds. The Common Crane is far from common in Britain, but is making a remarkable comeback after being extinct here for 400 years. In 1979 a few birds started to appear in East Anglia, and helped by careful habitat management on nature reserves and some reintroductions on the Somerset Levels, their numbers expanded across the south of England. In 2023, eighty pairs of cranes were recorded, and they successfully reared at least thirty-six chicks. Recently they have nested successfully at Willow Tree Fen, a new wetland reserve created from grazing lands acquired by the Lincolnshire Wildlife Trust. It's a bit of a detour from the Fosse Way, but easy to find, south of Lincoln near Spalding.

The crane is the UK's tallest bird, and is known for its extravagant bonding ritual. Pairs throw back their black, white and red heads, and emit loud squawking sounds called trumpeting, while flapping their wings and excitedly dancing up and down. In January they will form flocks of up to 40 birds roosting together, returning to their nesting areas in March. But you might see them passing over The Fens at any time of year, and at Willow Tree Fen there is a new raised viewing area where you can scan the wet fields and reed beds, and the wide Lincolnshire skies above.

Our journey along the Fosse Way from its junction with Ermin Street in Lincoln to the sea in Devon begins south of the Lincoln hill along Sincil Bank, with the road following a dyke across the flood plain of the River Witham. The dyke was almost certainly cut by the Romans. 'Sincil' in Old English means Big Ditch. Sincil Bank has been adopted as the name of the nearby Lincoln City football ground. To the left is a large area of parkland and scrub called South Common, with tinkling winter flocks of goldfinches and linnets prising seeds from the thistles and teasels. And on the other side of the common, a tall memorial spire marks the site of the International Bomber Command Centre.

The Perils of Bomber Command

It's a museum commemorating all the aircrew who died on the dangerous bombing raids to Germany in WWII, but it also tells stories of those who suffered as a result of the bombing campaigns. The international title of the centre emphasises that men and woman from no fewer than 62 countries served in Bomber Command, and the airmen who climbed into the Lancasters and Wellingtons to fly into Germany, many from airfields in Lincolnshire, all volunteered to do so.

It was incredibly perilous. About 60,000 aircrew were killed, with another 16,000 injured or captured. The missions at this time of year were particularly gruelling and hazardous, navigating in pitch darkness and intense cold, with the constant threat of German night fighters; the chances of surviving a full series of missions was about fifty-fifty. The average age of those killed was just 23. So it is hardly surprising that the annual service of remembrance at the spire monument attracts large crowds of service personnel, relatives and descendants from far and wide.

Leaving Lincoln along the Fosse Way to the south-west along Sincil Bank, we find ourselves on Newark

Road - unsurprisingly it aims directly to Newark – joining the A46 just outside the city. To the right is Whisby Nature Park. This is a fabulous nature reserve converted from disused gravel pits, and now managed by the Lincolnshire Wildlife Trust, with large lakes, reed beds, woodland, marsh and scrub. It has well-maintained paths and hides overlooking the main pools. In the summer the reserve is alive with warblers, finches and sand martins. In the depths of winter it is known for its murmurations of starlings and its brilliant wildfowl.

Whistling Ducks

Even before you reach the path by the water, you can hear from the whistling that there are wintering ducks to be seen, all dressed in their colourful breeding plumage. Apart from the familiar mallard, the most noticeable ducks are the wigeon. The males are gorgeous, with chestnut heads, golden brows, rippling grey feathers on the back, and black and white flashes on the wing that show up in flight. The females are browner; they have to stay camouflaged when sitting on the nest. The wigeon have flown a long way to be here. Their main breeding area is Northern Russia. They will be heading back there in a couple of months time after feeding up for the long journey. They like to graze on the grassy fringes of lakes and the characteristic whistle will always tell you if wigeon are around.

From the hides you can have good views of plenty of other ducks showing off their very best breeding plumage. The teal, our smallest duck species, are particularly handsome, with the drake flaunting his chestnut and green head, and under his tail there's a bright yellow triangle bordered in black. On the wing the flash of brilliant bluish-green was first recorded as a specific colour in 1917, and has since been adopted by Dulux and others - 'teal'. They also whistle, but with a more musical, fluting quality than the wigeon, rather like the sound of a penny-whistle. They breed in Siberia, and fly to northern Europe in the autumn to escape the harsh winter conditions there. If disturbed they spring into the air almost vertically, so the collective noun for these little ducks is a 'spring' of teal.

And on the far side of the main lake is a much rarer whistling duck that migrates to Britain in the winter from northern Russia. The pintail is the elegant aristocrat of the duck tribe. Both male and female are elongated, with long slim necks and the pointed tail after which it is named. The male has a milk-chocolate-coloured head with a fancy white stripe down the neck leading to a bright white chest, rippling feathers on the back, and black and white wing markings. The pintail is a stunner. Other wildfowl on the reserve are gadwall, with finely patterned grey plumage, and the ubiquitous Canada geese.

Foul Fowl?

Originally from the Kamchatka Peninsular in eastern Siberia and parts of China, as well as North America, Canada geese were introduced into northern Europe in the early 17th century by an explorer called Samuel de Champlain, who sent several pairs of geese to France as a present for King Louis XIII. It seems the royals liked these striking birds from far-flung lands, with their black necks and white chin-straps. A few were brought to Britain as an addition to King James II's collection of waterfowl in St. James' Park, and they gradually spread into the wild across the British Isles. They were pretty uncommon until the 20th century when the UK population exploded, probably because of the post-war expansion of arable farming and a decline in shooting. In 1953 there were only three or four thousand breeding in Britain and Ireland. Today the RSPB estimates a population of 190,000.

Many are semi-tame feral birds that lounge about in our parks waiting to be fed or picking up left-overs, and they are widely regarded as a pest. The Daily Mail columnist, Robert Hardman, called the Canada goose, 'the most loathsome bird in Britain'. The problem is their droppings. Goose poo contains some nasty bacteria that you don't want to get on your toddler's hands, and it can pollute pools, stifling the growth of water plants. Hardman says each bird produces droppings once every 40 seconds. Was he timing them? But certainly the Wildlife Trusts and local authorities have to spend a lot of effort cleaning up the paths and grassy areas in their reserves and parks. I suggest that we should never feed them, so they would have to move off to graze in the open fields.

Who Do You Think You Are, Walt Disney?

A couple of miles further down the A46 there are signs to the left to the small village of Norton Disney. In 1949 it had a surprise visit by the word famous movie-mogul, Walt Disney, who had already won 12 Oscars for films including Snow White and Fantasia. He had taken a break from supervising the filming of Treasure Island, to see if he could trace some English ancestors in this hamlet with the Disney name. He knew that his great-grandfather was Irish, but could the family have come originally from Lincolnshire? He was not disappointed.

According to the French Disney historian, Sebastian Durand, who was interviewed in 2023 by the BBC's Colin Paterson as part of the 100th anniversary of Disney films, Walt and members of his family arrived in the village in a convoy of cars, and spent the afternoon strolling round, taking photos, playing darts in the pub with the locals, and inspecting gravestones. It was in St. Peter's Church that he made the most significant discovery. The minister at the time, The Rev. R.K. Roper, told him that the De Isignys had been part of William the Conqueror's invasion force at the Battle of Hastings in 1066, and had been rewarded with an allocation of land south of Lincoln. Over centuries, the name had changed to d'Isigny, then d'Iseny, and eventually became Disney in the late Middle Ages. Walt also saw the rather grand 14th century tomb of Sir William d'Isney on which there was a family crest, with three lions facing left – the symbol of Normandy.

Durand says, "We know that the Disney name began in France, continued in England and went to Ireland, and then to America, so all people who share that name, including Walt Disney, share the same history. And the name comes from here". The famous animator was clearly delighted. In 1965, for the 10th anniversary of the Disneyland theme park in California, Walt wanted to add a coat of arms to Sleeping Beauty's castle, and he remembered the crest on the tomb in Norton Disney. Now the three lions on a shield are above the entrance to every Disney castle, and since 2006 it has appeared in the opening animation of every Disney film on the banner flying above the battlements of the fairy-tale castle - a tribute to a small English village. And here's an interesting detail. In the Lincolnshire archives there's a charter signed in 1386 that describes the name of the Disney family estate as 'Disnayland'.

A Mystery Object

In April 2024 Norton Disney again made headlines, this time it was a mystery dating back to its Roman origins. Put on display in the Lincoln Museum was a hollow dodecahedron, a carefully crafted copper alloy object with round apertures on the twelve sides, and bobbles like marbles welded on at the corners. A little larger than a cricket ball, it is one of the biggest of 33 found in Britain, and the only one to be discovered in the Midlands. It was found along with pottery from 1,700 years ago by local archeologists excavating a burial pit on a hill beside the village. It had been carefully placed there and is in perfect condition. Roman dodecahedra are regarded as one of archeology's great enigmas. Despite extensive research, no one knows what they were for! The TV archeologist, Alice Roberts, featured the Norton Disney object in 'Digging for Britain', and said, "It has to be one of the greatest, most mysterious, archaeological objects I've ever had the opportunity to look at." Suggestions for what the metal ball was used for poured in from viewers. They included, a spaghetti measuring device, a maths teaching aid, an incense burner, and a device used for knitting or crochet work. Architectural historian, Dr. Jonathan Foyle, favours the theory that the dodecahedron was used for framing the constellations of the zodiac. Dr Foyle said, "If you look through them you can frame a view - much like a camera operator." Explaining his theory, the broadcaster said the Romans had brought with them an understanding of the 12-sided universe described by Plato. He points out that a dodecahedron found in Switzerland in 1982 had the names of the 12 zodiac signs engraved on it. I'm not so sure. The fine metalwork is thought to be Celtic, so perhaps even the Romans didn't know what these metal balls were. The secretary of the Norton Disney Archeology Group said, "Magic, rituals or religion? We may never know."

Counting the Birds

Continuing south-west along the A46 Fosse Way, we slip into Nottinghamshire. In fact for a mile or so near Collingham the county border follows the Fosse Way itself. Approaching Newark, a short distance to the right up the A1133 we find another lovely nature reserve created from former gravel workings. In mid-winter, the RSPB reserve of Langford Lowfields has marsh harriers quartering the reed beds with their broad wings held in a shallow v-shape, plenty of wintering waders and wildfowl, water rails grunting and pip-pipping from the reeds, and spectacular murmurations of starlings on cold, clear evenings. The reserve is also a noted haunt of the elusive bittern. This skulking member of the heron family has made a terrific comeback from near extinction thanks to the efforts of conservationists. Bitterns can be very difficult to count, because they stay in the reed beds, where they stand with bills pointing to the sky and their streaked plumage is perfect camouflage. But they can be heard if not seen. At dawn and dusk in the spring, the males seeking a mate 'boom'. The sound is more of a foghorn-like 'hoom' than a boom, and can be heard three miles away, making it the loudest bird in the UK. So naturalists count the number of booming males to estimate the number of pairs in the country.

In 1997, conservationists counted just 11 booming males in England and Wales. Since then, restoration of their reed bed habitat has allowed the species to recover, with more than 230 calling males counted in recent breeding seasons. Simon Wotton, an RSPB senior scientist, says, "Many wetlands were drained in the 19th and 20th centuries to make space for agriculture, leaving the bittern with fewer and fewer places to breed. One of the aims of the bittern work since 1990 was to create or restore suitable wetlands away from the coast – safe sites that wouldn't be affected by the impacts of climate change, such as rising sea levels. Rewetting these spaces also helps prevent flooding and fights the climate crisis; wetlands are incredible carbon sponges." It would be an exaggeration to say that numbers of this elusive bird are booming - the bittern is amber-listed, meaning the species is still under threat - but it is doing well, thanks to the dedicated work of conservationists working to restore wetlands across the central belt of England.

Most birdwatchers keep lists. I am no exception. I have a Life List of species seen, a British List, a Garden List and a few Holiday Lists, and I usually keep a Year List. It's always fun to start from scratch on New Year's Day and see if I can beat the previous year's number of species. So I find myself making a Fosse Way List version of my Year List. I should get to 100 as the seasons change, especially since the route ends at a river estuary and the sea, with the prospect of quite a few species that aren't seen inland. I've chalked up 50 birds already, and mentally set a target for the year of double that number.

Brough

Further along the A46 Fosse Way is the hamlet of Brough. It stands on the site of a Roman town with the unlikely name of of Crococalana, which grew around a military fort in the 1st century AD. Archeologists reckon the town spread along the Roman Fosse Way for about a mile, and had ditched defences. It was one of a series of significant forts along the fossa to protect Roman-controlled England in the early years following the invasion of AD 43.

It seems the Brough name, though unusual, has no connection with the Brough motorcycles made in nearby Nottingham by George Brough in the twenties and thirties. At the time, these motorbikes were the fastest in the world, and at about £300 per machine - that's about £10,000 in modern currency - they were expensive, but they had some cachet. George Bernard Shaw rode one. So did Lawrence of Arabia who owned seven of them, and died crashing one into a tree. These days a Brough Superior from the nineteen twenties could set you back a quarter of a million pounds.

Newark and the Trent

Approaching Newark on the A46, a sign to the left points us to the Newark Air Museum on the site of a WWII training airfield. It's an extensive and well-presented outdoor and indoor display of 90 aircraft covering the complete history of aviation, from flimsy early flying machines to a huge Vulcan bomber, the Typhoon Eurofighter, and many more military and civilian planes and helicopters. Visiting children can get the chance to climb into a cockpit, and imagine they are Top Gun.

The Fosse Way goes right through the middle of Newark, or to give this historic market town its full title, Newark-on-Trent. To my mind it is underrated as a destination to visit, perhaps because it is eclipsed by the better-known county towns of Nottingham, Leicester and Lincoln not far away. Newark has a rich history, and is extremely attractive, with a mixture of medieval, Elizabethan, Georgian and Victorian buildings, an elegant market square, and an impressive semi-ruined castle overlooking the river. The stone castle was constructed by the Norman invaders, but Newark's original fort was Roman. The location is at the junction of the Fosse and The Great North Road, now the A1, built by the Romans, probably on the line of an ancient trackway. And this chosen site for a fortified town was on the River Trent, an important waterway.

Celtic Gold

While the original fortified settlement here dates from the first century, there's plenty of evidence of human activity well before the Romans arrived. The Newark Museum's collection has pottery, axe heads and sword blades from the bronze age and iron age found along the course of the river. In 2005, a tree surgeon called Maurice Richardson was metal-detecting on the outskirts of Newark when his detector started beeping loudly. He had to dig down quite a long way until he pulled out a fabulous gold torc – a heavy neckband, eight inches across. The body is formed from rolled gold alloy wires mixed with silver and copper, which had been plaited into eight thin ropes, then twisted together. The terminals are ring-shaped with floral designs. I wonder if Maurice danced on the spot as detectorists are supposed to do when they find gold.

The torc has been dated to between 250 BC and 50 BC. The Head of Research at the British Museum, Jeremy Hill, said, "It's probably the most significant find of Iron Age Celtic gold jewellery made in the last 50 years ... it shows an incredibly high level of technological skill in working the metal and a really high level of artistry. It is an extraordinary object." The Newark Torc can be seen in the town's Millgate Museum, though it's sometimes on loan to the British Museum in London. For the so-called Ancient Britons of the East Midlands of England, the River Trent must have been an invaluable transport highway through the heavily wooded countryside, allowing them to travel to mainland Europe and trade their furs, cloth and manufactured goods for gold.

At 185 miles long, the Trent is the UK's third longest river, after the Severn and the Thames, flowing north-east from Staffordshire into the Humber estuary and giving access to the North Sea trading routes. In former times, Newark was a thriving inland port. A tributary of the Trent, the River Devon, runs into the main river on the south side of town, and then the Trent splits into three channels running over a series of weirs called locally the Newark Waterfalls. It's a tranquil, photogenic location, with tree-lined banks, and grey wagtails and kingfishers flashing past, as well as the usual ducks and swans. In sheltered spots there are clumps of nodding snowdrops. But Newark's history has been far from tranquil. Over the centuries there have been various violent struggles over who would have control of the castle and therefore of the surrounding lands.

Sieges and Civil War

In the thirteenth century, Robert de Gaugy, a Norman baron with a private army, was given custody of Newark Castle by King John. After the King's death at the castle from dysentery, a year after he had signed Magna Carta, the baron was ordered to hand over the fortress to its rightful owner, the Bishop of Lincoln. De Gaugy refused point-blank. Contemporary accounts describe the baron as 'bad', 'truculent' and 'defiant'. The Earl Marshall, with the boy king, nine-year old Henry III, accompanying him, and supported by the forces of the Dauphin of France, besieged the castle using great stone-throwing engines called mangonels. They didn't make much impression on the huge walls and after eight days, 'Bad' Robert was paid £100 to leave with his freebooters; but according to a chronicler, he died soon afterwards, 'smitten with the infernal fire'.

Three hundred years later it was The English Civil Wars that brought more conflict to the castle walls. Newark was a Royalist stronghold with King Charles I based for a while at nearby Nottingham. The castle was besieged three times towards the end of the First Civil War in 1644 and 1645, but each time the Parliamentarians were repelled by around 600 defending troops. In the summer of 1645, Newark cavalry rode off to fight with the King's forces at the decisive Battle of Naseby. Outnumbered by the 'ironclads' led by Thomas Fairfax and Oliver Cromwell, they were heavily defeated and survivors had to retire to the safety of the castle. The following year, the defeated King Charles had to order the garrison to surrender, which they did under protest, and much of the defences of the town, including parts of the castle were dismantled. You can follow the story of this shameful and deadly period in British history at the National Civil War Centre at Newark's Appleton Gate. There are weapons, armour, and other artefacts that tell the tale of England's civil revolution that culminated in the beheading of the king, 144 years before France was convulsed by a similar trauma, and King Louis XVI and Queen Marie Antoinette were to lose their heads. But in England, after all the bloodshed, the monarchy was restored by popular demand after just eleven years.

February

Nottingham to Leicester

'Pass through this brief patch of time in harmony with Nature'
(Marcus Aurelius)

Red Kite

Towards Nottingham

Leaving Newark southwards on the A46, the Farndon roundabout is where the dual carriageway, opened in 2012, diverges slightly from the original Roman road, called, unsurprisingly, Fosse Road. The old road runs in parallel with the A46 perfectly straight for 5 miles along the valley of the Trent. The sign to Farndon to the right takes us to a lovely little nature reserve by the river called Farndon Ponds. In fact it's one large pond with pleasure boats and plenty of wildfowl, with a circular walk through woodland and grassland. At this time of year the birds have paired up, with the great-crested grebes shaking their heads at each other as a prelude to their elaborate mating dances, when the grebes stand up in the water offering each other a bouquet of weeds. Or sometimes the male will approach his intended partner underwater, then pop up in front of her, head shaking madly, saying, "Surprise! Here I am!"

There are coloured information boards with maps of the trails round the reserve, and just along the river bank is the Fardon Ferry bar and bistro, with views across the Trent and outdoor dining when the weather is warmer. It's named after an ancient ferry crossing. The Farndon Ferry is mentioned in documents from 1583, and until fifty years ago a ferry still operated across the Trent from Farndon to Rolleston on the north bank. An act of bravery at the ferry in 1948 is still celebrated locally. Twelve year old Ronnie Ward from Newark earned the title of 'The Little Hero of Farndon', when he swam out to rescue a four year old boy who had been swept into deep water. He pulled the child to a landing stage where he could be carried back to his mother. Ronnie's parents knew nothing about the rescue until they heard the story from neighbours who had watched the drama; their son had been too modest to tell them.

The Last Battle of the Roses Wars

A short distance down the Fosse Road we find the hamlet of East Stoke, population 152. You could have no idea that this peaceful spot was the scene of one of the bloodiest battles in British history. The Battle of Stoke Field in 1487 is regarded as the final battle of the Wars of the Roses that had lasted no fewer than 32 years, as the houses of Lancaster and York contested the throne of England. Two years earlier, the Yorkist army had been defeated at the Battle of Bosworth, with Richard III killed – according to Shakespeare, calling desperately for a horse to make his escape. Henry VII sought to end the long-running wars by marrying Elizabeth of York and combining the red rose and the white into the Tudor rose to create a new dynasty. But the Earl of Lincoln refused to give up his right to the crown. He was Richard III's nephew and had been chosen as his heir.

The story of the final battle involves a boy imposter, foreign mercenaries and a massacre that left the Trent running red with blood. The rebel Earl of Lincoln was introduced to a ten-year-old boy called Lambert Simnel. The son of a tradesman, he was said to have princely looks, and had been educated in courtly etiquette by a priest who was sympathetic to the Yorkists' cause. Lambert Simnel was the same age as another claimant to the throne, the young Earl of Warwick who was imprisoned in The Tower. When it was falsely rumoured that young Warwick had died, Lambert Simnel was taken to Dublin where he was presented as the escaped Earl of Warwick, crowned King Edward VI and paraded through the city. The Yorkist rebels recruited 4,500 Irish mercenaries and another 2,000 men were shipped in from Flanders. This considerable force landed with the Young Pretender in Lancashire, and gaining more fighters from sympathetic barons along the route, they marched south-east as fast as they could. King Henry had assembled 12,000 troops at Radcliffe east of Nottingham, and when he heard the Yorkists had forded the River Trent, he marched his men 8 miles down the Fosse Way to intercept them. He lined up the infantry on a low hill called Burham Furlong, just to the south of East Stoke village. Among them were an elite force of longbowmen from Wales.

The Irish mercenaries didn't have body armour, and volleys of arrows from the king's archers drove them into an area enclosed by a loop in the river; many were trapped in a sunken road known to this day as the Red Gutter or Bloody Gutter. Within three hours an estimated seven thousand men had been massacred, most of them Yorkists, with hundreds drowned in the Trent. The rebel Earl of Lincoln and other leading Yorkists were killed, but the boy imposter was pardoned, in recognition that he was just a puppet. The King brought him into the royal household where he worked in the kitchens as a spit-turner and later became a falconer. On the rising ground of Burham Furlong stands a large stone memorial with the carved legend, 'Here stood the Burrand Bush planted on the spot where Henry VII placed his standard after the Battle of Stoke June 16th 1487.'

Signs of early Spring

A few miles further down the A46 we reach the right turn into Nottingham, and there are signs to the Holme Pierrepont Country Park, home to the National Watersports Centre beside the river, with its two-kilometre rowing course and white water kayaking course. And next door is the Skylarks Nature Reserve created by the Nottinghamshire Wildlife Trust from former gravel pits, and notable because in 1982 it was the first in the country to be laid out specifically for wheelchair users. The weatherproof paths are particularly welcome this year following weeks of relentless rain that has left the ground saturated and with thick mud clogging many woodland trails. Here at Skylarks there's a two-mile footpath linking viewing screens and boardwalks that allow fantastic views of the lakes with their winter wildfowl, with woodlands, ponds, reed beds, meadows and scrapes, (shallow pools that attract waders). In early February the resident birds such as the mallard and tufted ducks have all paired up and some are already nesting in the waterside sedges. The coots are arguing over territories with their sharp pink-pink calls and engaging in occasional scraps, scrabbling at each other with their huge feet.

And there's another fabulous nature reserve just on the other side of Nottingham where the River Erewash joins the Trent. The Attenborough Reserve was opened by Sir David, but actually the name comes from a nearby village. It's an extensive area of wetland covering 350 acres of pools, reed beds, scrub and woodland. It used to be a site for extracting gravel, and is now owned and managed by the Nottinghamshire Wildlife Trust, with asphalt paths and a big educational centre with views across the reed beds. It's a good place to hear booming bitterns in the spring, and has recorded an impressive 250 bird species, including some extremely rare water birds such as the squacco heron, a native of southern Europe and Africa, and the sora rail from the Americas, probably caught in the increasingly frequent storm systems piling in across the Atlantic as the climate changes.

Getting Warmer

There are signs of the warming climate everywhere with daffodils in full bloom and plenty of pink blossom on the cherry plum trees. They were imported from Central Asia in the 16th century and are now common in English parks; they are often the first to blossom. And in the hedgerows, the blackthorn is already in flower. Traditionally the thorn bush blossoms were March and April for blackthorn and May for hawthorn, hence its country name, 'may'. But here we are in mid-February and the blackthorn is decorating the tops of the hedges with clouds of little white flowers. Lower down on the drier banks the gorse is covered in vivid golden blooms. There are three species of gorse in Britain. This is the early flowering common gorse. The dwarf gorse and western gorse won't come into flower until July.

The violent storms that swept across the country in January causing floods and travel disruption have passed, but a succession of Atlantic fronts have brought more rain and there is standing water on many of the nearby fields. It is very mild for the time of year and the occasional butterfly can be seen already – peacocks and brimstones that have hibernated over the winter. The air is full of birdsong. The song thrushes are belting out their sharp repetitive phrases, and the great tits are 'belling' their two-note spring song. I can hear a higher-pitched two-note call that can be confused with the great tit. This is the smaller coal tit. The call is more like a squeaky rubber toy being squeezed: 'see-saw, see-saw'.

So is spring really arriving earlier each year? It certainly is in southern England and Wales according to meteorologists and conservationists who monitor climate trends. The British Trust for Ornithology has reported a blackbird with a fledgling in early January and a great-crested grebe with young in the same month. A recent Royal Society report into plant flowering trends used more than 400,000 observations going back to the year 1753. It concluded that a 1.2 degree increase in global temperatures since then has brought spring forward by a full month. And it seems the trend is accelerating. Kathryn Brown, Director of Climate Action at the Wildlife Trusts, says the patterns are plain to see. "We know very clearly that spring is coming earlier and earlier every year, and that is due to climate change. There's a whole range of different impacts from a warming planet." She mentions the close relationships between ecosystems and species, and particularly the profound effect on the changing behaviour of insects - the pollinators and a major food source for so many creatures.

Mad about Saffron

In the shelter of the trees – what are these little purple and white shoots? They are crocuses, well into flower in February with patches of golden crocuses starting to appear across the open grass. The crocus is the county flower of Nottinghamshire. It's a beautiful little flower with a fascinating history. A member of the iris family of plants, the crocus group has about 100 different species, including the much prized *crocus sativus*. This has vivid crimson stigma and styles inside the petals, and from the beginning of recorded history these little flowers have been collected to make the spice, saffron.

It is used for seasoning, has numerous health benefits, and is a brilliant red dye. It is also extremely valuable. The saffron crocus, originally found across the Balkans, Asia and parts of the Middle East is no longer discovered in the wild, but is cultivated commercially in Greece, Kashmir, Turkey, and notably in Iran, which produces more than half of the world's saffron. Gathering saffron is very labour-intensive and is back-breaking work. To produce just one kilo of saffron, 150,000 flowers have to be hand picked, and their stigmas laid out to dry in the sun. That's a week's work for a picker. In western markets, that kilo of saffron can cost $10,000. An ounce of pure saffron is valued at more than an ounce of gold. So it's not surprising that there is plenty of fake or adulterated saffron around. Fake saffron can be corn silk threads, coconut filaments, dyed horse hair or even shredded paper. You can test the saffron you buy by soaking it in tepid water for a while; the dye used to colour fake saffron will soon come off.

City of Caves

It's just a short hop from the A46 Fosse Way into the city of Nottingham with its impressive Norman castle on a rise above the Trent; but the city's history reaches back much further in time. The Celtic 'Ancient Britons' lived here and called the place *Tigguo Cobauc*, which means 'a place of cave dwellings', because the sandstone cliff is riddled with a network of caves. Shortly after their invasion, the Romans built one of their major Fosse Way forts near Nottingham at a place they called *Margidunum*. But when their Empire fell apart and the legions were withdrawn, a Saxon chieftain with the unfortunate name of Snot ruled the area, which then became known as Snotingaham, meaning the home of Snot's people.

Now as a destination for a visit, Nottingham is not to be sniffed at. The 800 caves and tunnels beneath the city are a popular tourist attraction. At time of writing it will cost you a mere £8.75 to enjoy the UK's largest underground network - the 'City of Caves Experience' - where you'll hear about their use over the years as troglodyte homes, cellars for casks of wine, a tannery, air raid shelters, (Nottingham was bombed by the Luftwaffe in May 1941 with the loss of 178 lives), and their place in the exploits of Robin Hood.

Robin Hood

Around the world, Nottingham is known for the legend of Robin of Loxley, deprived of his lands by 'bad' King John when fighting in the crusades in support of Richard the Lionheart, and returning to live in Sherwood Forest as an outlaw with his Merrie Men. Who hasn't heard of Friar Tuck, the seven-foot-tall Little John, Will Scarlet, Alan-a-Dale, Much the Miller's Son, and the rest, with the romantic interest introduced in the 15th century in the form of Maid Marian. It's a cracking tale that began as a popular ballad according to old manuscripts, but has been embroidered many times over the centuries. When Robin wasn't robbing the rich to give to the poor, he was bravely escaping and releasing captives from Nottingham Castle by cunningly using the cave network under its foundations, with his skill as an archer and swashbuckling swordsman getting him out of many a tight spot. There have been well over a hundred depictions of the tale of Robin Hood on stage, the big screen and TV. Here are just a few of the actors who have taken on the role of the outlaw clad in Lincoln green - in no particular order:

Douglas Fairbanks, the thigh-slapping Errol Flynn, Richard Todd, Patrick Troughton when he wasn't being a Time Lord, the aptly named Richard Greene, (I'm old enough to remember his hugely popular ITV series), Frank Sinatra, Kevin Costner with his full-on American accent, Russell Crowe, Margaret Rutherford (honestly), Frankie Howerd and Kermit the Frog. There are many more and no doubt there will be in the future.

Nottingham has benefitted hugely from Robin's worldwide fame. Thousands of tourists visit the city specifically to walk in the footsteps of the legendary hero. I've counted two dozen Robin Hood attractions, and it seems every other shop around the Market Square has souvenirs of the legendary hero. The castle offers a guided tour of the caves and tunnels, and an immersive Robin Hood exhibition. Outside the walls there is a famous bronze statue erected in 1949, and now the subject of thousands of photographs and selfies. Robin is aiming his arrow at the gatehouse where the Sheriff's men would emerge. Unfortunately the arrow has been stolen several times, and has had to be replaced. From the castle you can take the Robin Hood Trail round the city, with 12 noticeboards at significant locations, including where in disguise he won the Sheriff's golden arrow, and the church where he and Marian were married.

The Major Oak

You can also take a bus ride for about 50 minutes north of Nottingham to Sherwood Forest, where there is a visitor centre, nature trails and the Major Oak, regularly voted Britain's favourite tree, and said to be where the Merrie Men would sleep among its branches. It is massive, with the spreading limbs supported by a circle of poles. Its age isn't known precisely but it would certainly have been a very big tree 800 years ago. Apparently more than 350,000 tourists go to see it every year.

But wait a moment. Dare I whisper that Robin Hood probably didn't exist? And if he was a real person, did he not hail from Yorkshire? Historians and researchers have argued about this for centuries. Robin or Robert Hood was a relatively common name, and pops up occasionally in court records all over the midlands and north. Loxley estate was just outside modern day Sheffield, and was first referred to as the birthplace of Robin Hood in the seventeenth century, 400 years after the reign of Richard I. Certainly there are earlier written references to the folk legend, but no evidence that Robin and his band ever really existed. But don't mention it when you visit Nottingham. The tourist industry has been a significant economic buffer as the city's traditional employers of lace-making, mining, Raleigh bicycles, Boots the chemists and the Players cigarette factory declined.

As a footnote to the Robin Hood phenomenon, it is worth recalling that in 1953 during the American post-war paranoia about the threat of Communism, a school commission board member in Indiana called Mrs. White proposed a ban on the stories. "There is now a Communist directive in education to stress the story of Robin Hood. They want to stress it because he stole from the rich and gave to the poor. That's the Communist line." In response to the attempt to ban Robin Hood, a group of college students went to a poultry farm, collected feathers, and dyed them green to represent the one worn by Robin. Calling themselves the 'Merry Outlaws' they pinned the feathers around their campuses, and published pamphlets against McCarthyism and censorship. The 'Green Feather Movement' spread and before long the witch hunts by Senator McCarthy had run out of steam as more and more Americans saw the attacks on 'unpatriotic' films and books as ludicrous hysteria.

The Wolds

Back on the A46 Fosse Way, the road travels as straight as one of Robin Hood's arrows into Leicestershire at Willoughby on the Wolds. The name 'wolds' comes from the Anglo-Saxon for woods, but became known as the cleared upland areas in the forests. They are rolling hills on the great seam of limestone and chalk that runs under the Fosse, with clefts where the rivers and streams have cut though. There are 'wolds' in Lincolnshire, Yorkshire and of course the Cotswolds, but the name is most often attached to The Wolds of the East Midlands covering parts of Nottinghamshire and Leicestershire and stretching east to Rutland Water. It's open country with large fields of cereal crops, as described in the opening lines of Tennyson's 'Lady of Shalott'.

> *On either side the river lie*
> *Long fields of barley and of rye,*
> *That clothe the wold and meet the sky.*

The Wolds are also kite country.

The Fabulous Red Kite

The return of the red kite in recent years has been a spectacular conservation success story. In Shakespeare's time kites were common, scavenging over towns and cities, but by the early 1800s, through shooting and trapping on country estates, they had become extinct in England with just a few pairs hanging on in Wales. The Welsh birds weren't hatching many young, partly as a result of eating poisoned carrion, and there was also concern about low genetic diversity. So the RSPB and Natural England launched an ambitious plan to introduce birds from mainland Europe. In July 1990, 13 red kites were flown in by British Airways from Spain. They had been taken from nests at the age of about 4 weeks, kept in large pens and fed on the kind of carrion they might find in the wild. During the next few years a total of 90 young birds from Spain and Scandinavia were released, first in the Chilterns and Scotland, then in the East Midlands. Today there are more than 10,000 red kites in Britain. Tony Juniper from Natural England says, "In a few short decades we have taken a species from the brink of extinction in the UK to being home to almost 10% of the entire world population. It might be the biggest species success story in UK conservation history."

One of our oldest native species of raptor, the red kite is a magnificent bird. With a wingspan of more than six feet, it's larger than a buzzard. It is richly patterned in streaked ginger, with white and black on the wings, a pale head, and the characteristic red forked tail that twitches as it rides the air currents. Kites are a regular sight soaring over the Fosse Way looking for road kill. They have keen eyesight and it's thought they might have a decent sense of smell. Certainly when I was at an outdoor event in Oxfordshire recently, there were tables with sandwiches laid out, and I noticed a kite cruising above us, and within a few minutes there were six kites watching us from above. They probably fancied a ham and cheese sandwich with its crusts cut off, but they kept their distance.

Feeding the kites has become quite popular in some parts, with farmers and people with large gardens leaving out food so that they can see these great birds at close range. But the RSPB urges people not to leave out food for kites. It can only encourage the birds to think that a child holding a sandwich might be offering a treat! And let me bust one myth. Social media posts have said owners of cats and small dogs are afraid to let them out in case Tiddles or their much-loved Pomeranian is taken by a kite. As far as I can discover, there is no credible evidence that kites carry off cats or toy dogs. Kites live substantially on carrion, but will take voles, mice or rats if they have the chance.

Naming the Birds

In medieval times, the red kite was known as a 'glead'. In fact most of our common birds had different names and there were many regional differences, so as interest in the natural world grew in the seventeenth century, scientists reported 'widespread confusion' between the species. Here are a few of the traditional names of birds used in the English midlands.

Ars-foot	Great Crested Grebe
Bald Buzzard	Osprey
Bastard Plover	Lapwing
Didapper	Little Grebe
Ox-eye	Great Tit
Puttock	Common Buzzard
Woodspite	Green Woodpecker

In the seventeenth century, a Cambridge University tutor called John Ray and his student Francis Willughby set about classifying as many species as they could, travelling widely, dissecting specimens and making detailed drawings. But Willughby suffered from ill-health and in 1672 died at the age of just thirty-six. Five years later Ray had compiled all their joint findings and published 'Ornithology', the first detailed catalogue of the birds of Northern Europe, with Latin names that exist to this day, and common names adapted from Anglo-Saxon such as redstart (red-tail) or wheatear (white-arse). Since then many more species have been identified, some with names that describe them, (blackcap, whitethroat), some named after their preferred habitat, (reed warbler, marsh tit), others from their calls, (chiffchaff, cuckoo), and some from the ornithologists who first identified them as a distinct species, (Montague's harrier, Bewick swan). There's an excellent book by Tim Birkhead called 'The Wonderful Mr. Willughby – the first true ornithologist', with much of the information based on the Willughby family archive lodged in the Nottingham University library.

Pies

Down the A46 at Six Hills, there's a junction signed to Melton Mowbray. But you can look for the six hills in vain. There are one or two pre-historic barrows nearby, but the landscape is a plateau. As with the names of many hamlets in England, when the Normans came to write down the place-names, they wrote how it sounded when spoken by the locals. On early maps the name is shown as 'Seggs or Segs Hill' (singular). Some antiquarian commentators have proposed that 'seggs' is a corruption of a dialect word for sheep. The Ancient Britons were trading wool across the channel well before the Roman invasion.

A short diversion to the left takes us to the so-called capital of The Wolds, Melton Mowbray, on the River Eye. It is famed worldwide for its pork pies. It's also the home of one of six licensed makers of Stilton cheese, produced at the Tuxford and Tebbutt Creamery, and the town is promoted as England's 'Rural Capital of Food'. In Roman times, Melton, as it's known locally, benefitted from being near the garrisoned forts and camps along the Fosse Way, supplying the troops with food. By the time of the Norman invasion and the 1086 Domesday Book, it was an established centre of trade with two markets per week, the only markets in the county, and two water mills. Historical evidence suggests they've been making blue-veined cheese here for centuries. The whey from the cheesemaking was fed to pigs and as a result Melton pork was fine quality.

In 1851 John Dickinson opened a bakery in Nottingham Street just off the Market Square, and his Grandma, Mary Dickinson, began making pork pies, using a wooden dolly to hand-raise the pastry into cup-shapes, then introducing jelly to protect and preserve the meat inside. The pies immediately became popular with members of the famous Leicestershire Quorn Hunt, who could pop a couple of pies into their saddlebags, and soon the fine pork pies were in demand far and wide. When Joseph Morris joined the expanding firm in

1886, the famous brand of Dickinson and Morris came about. Today Ye Olde Pork Pie Shoppe on the site of the original bakery still produces hand-made pies. In 2008 the European Union awarded the Melton Mowbray pork pie 'Protected Geographical Indication' status. Only pies made in a designated zone round Melton using uncured pork may bear the Melton Mowbray name. Now part of the Samworth Brothers food business, nearby factories produce thousands of pies each day, supplying all the main supermarket chains. And a tip from Dickinson and Morris – they believe the most flavoursome pies have greyish meat, which is fresh and uncured. In pies made from cured pork the meat is pink.

More Lakes and Parkland

The A607 Melton Road brings us back to the ruler-straight Fosse Way to the north of the city of Leicester, and to the right just outside the ring road is a beautiful nature reserve created on a series of pools in the valley of the River Soar. It's called the Watermead Country Park, run by the City Council and Leicestershire County Council, and it covers 340 acres of reed beds, woodland, meadows and trails. Just across a tributary of the Soar called the River Wreake, there are the Cossington Lakes, an extensive wetland alive with waterfowl at this time of year. And what on earth is that across the water, standing on a low hill? It's a woolly mammoth! In fact it's a life-sized sculpture of a mammoth made of concrete and steel. It overlooks the flooded gravel pit where the remains of an Ice Age woolly mammoth were found, and is now popular with children who can climb up its giant tusks.

There's a wide range of bird life here with herons, cormorants and grebes along with the usual ducks and geese just a couple of miles from a population centre. And they also have tree sparrows. These are close cousins of our well-known house sparrows, but in many ways they are different. For a start, they are much less common. Leicestershire is a stronghold, but to the north and west of England they are scarce. Unlike the house sparrow, the male and female look the same and they mate for life. The tree sparrow is a very attractive little bird with a chestnut crown and nape, a black bib and a black triangle on each white cheek. Across the UK the tree sparrow population has plummeted, estimated by the RSPB to have fallen by 93% in the past sixty years. No one knows why, but this is a bird of the countryside, shyer than the house sparrow, so like many other farmland birds such as skylarks and corn buntings, it has probably been affected by the reduced food supply caused by intensive agricultural practices. However, recent Breeding Bird Survey data suggests that tree sparrow numbers may have started to recover slightly. It's certainly encouraging to find a nesting colony in the woodland fringe at Watermead, so close to the centre of Leicester.

March

Leicestershire into Warwickshire

"Through astrology and the study of the heavens men may
approach very near to the power of the gods."
(Cicero, 'On Divination')

House Sparrows

The Cheeky Sparrow

On the Fosse Way that spears straight into the centre of the city of Leicester, the tree sparrows' more plentiful cousins, the house sparrows, seem to enjoy playing chicken on the busy road. Small chirruping flocks are picking up insects that have been hit by passing vehicles, and as you drive towards them they seem to leave it to the very last second before they fly into the nearest hedge. There are plenty of dead birds along our main roads – wood pigeons, pheasants and crows, for example - but I haven't seen many corpses of sparrows. The audacious house sparrow seems to be just a bit more agile.

This familiar little bird is one of the commonest across the world. But strangely its numbers have been suffering from a quite steep decline. In the UK, populations have fallen by about 70% in the past 50 years. This loss of house sparrows hit the headlines about thirty years ago when Londoners started noticing the absence of sparrows in their parks. What had happened to the cheeky cockney sparrow adopted as the bird of the capital city? Various theories were bandied about. Some thought that the increase in urban sparrowhawks was to blame. I think that's a pretty ridiculous notion. It would take huge numbers of sparrowhawks to decimate the sparrow population. And predators never eliminate their main prey species, for obvious reasons. And the loss of the house sparrow was happening everywhere. It largely vanished from Karachi, Mumbai and New Delhi. Some blamed electromagnetic radiation from mobile phone masts, with little or no evidence.

I suspect a combination of a decline in the availability of insect food during the breeding season, poor air quality in cities, and a virus. There are many infections affecting birds. We know something about the bird flu that affects poultry, wildfowl and seabirds. And we know that sparrows are particularly vulnerable to mites, ticks and lice. The latest theory advanced by researchers in North America suggests the birds may have been afflicted by a form of avian malaria carried by mosquitos. Blood samples taken from house sparrow showed a high incidence of the disease. But whatever the reason for their recent decline, it seems that numbers are starting to recover, and the house sparrow is still the commonest garden bird according to the RSPB's annual Great Garden Birdwatch.

In 2005, one house sparrow achieved international fame, and was named 'The Domino Sparrow'. In the Expo Centre at Leeuwarden in the Netherlands, preparations were underway for an attempt on the world record for toppling dominoes. It would be televised live. More than 4 million domino bricks had been carefully lined up. A female house sparrow got into the hall and landed on a domino which toppled 43,000 bricks until they met a safety gap, made just in case of an accident. A hunter was hired to get rid of the intruder. Having failed to catch the sparrow in a net, he pulled out his gun and shot it. There was public outrage. A radio DJ offered 3,000 euros to anyone who would topple the dominoes before the event. Scores of security guards were hired to seal off the hall. Animal rights organisations took to court the company that provided the 'hunter' and the TV production company, Endemol. The shooter was fined 200 euros for killing a protected wild bird. The now famous sparrow was stuffed at the Natural History Museum in Rotterdam where you can still see the little bird that holds the avian world record for toppling dominoes.

Spuds and Space

Before we enter Leicester, there are a couple of places on the north side of the city worthy of a visit. Just outside the ring road is one of the biggest local employers. It was started in a small way just after the second world war by a local butcher called Henry Walker. With meat rationing still in force he was looking for another product to keep the business alive, and settled on spuds. He began hand-slicing and frying potatoes to make crisps that were sprinkled with salt and sold at threepence a bag – or a 'thrupenny-bit', (that's just over 1p in modern currency).

Today the Walkers Crisp production factory is the largest in the world with a wide range of flavours. In the fifties, cheese and onion was designed to replicate the ploughman's lunch. Then salt and vinegar was inspired by the nation's love of fish and chips, prawn cocktail paid tribute to the popular '70s starter, and roast chicken flavour was based on the Sunday roast. You can book a tour of one of the Walkers factories and see how they produce a whopping 13 million packets of crisps every day. But these days they cost a bit more than a thrupenny-bit per packet.

And just off the Fosse Way on the north side of Leicester is another big attraction that is somewhat less down to earth than potato crisps. It's the National Space Centre, opened in 2001 in partnership with the University of Leicester, and immediately popular with visitors from across the country – around 400,000 a year at the last count. That's hardly surprising. Approaching the site there is the enormous rocket tower, home to Blue Streak and Thor Able rockets, as well as the Gagarin Experience, Apollo Lunar Lander and some real Moon Rock. Four exhibition decks tell the story of the Space Race, the history of rocketry, and Britain's involvement in space exploration. There's also a fabulous planetarium. Unfortunately modern light pollution in our cities means that most of us don't see the heavens in the same way as the ancients did.

The Romans who built the Fosse Way must have enjoyed brilliant star-scapes, unaffected by atmospheric pollution or electric light. They studied the night sky, navigated by it, loved it and worshipped it. The heavens were regarded as the gateway to the world of the gods. To this day the planets and stars are named after Roman deities. The giant planet Jupiter is the Roman god of the sky and thunder, the king of the Roman gods. Mars is the god of war and Venus the goddess of love. Mercury was the swift messenger and considered the most intelligent of the deities. Saturn was the god of agriculture, and Neptune the god of the oceans. And it wasn't just the planets, all visible celestial bodies including asteroids were named after deities, such as the giant asteroid composed of particularly reflective rock that represents Vesta, the goddess of purity, hearth and home.

Their fascination didn't end with the scientific study of planetary activity. The Romans believed the night sky could illuminate their personal destiny - the origin of the horoscopes still popular in some tabloid newspapers. Until the 17th century, there wasn't the distinction we see today between astronomy and astrology. Ancient beliefs that the heavens conferred the ability to foretell the future aren't surprising when you consider that a deep knowledge of the stars and planets helped predict the seasons, the tides, and when to harvest, and guided by the night sky Romans navigated their empire. In fact astronomy was at the centre of Roman culture, politics, religious belief and philosophical thought, and helped to shape the course of human history for thousands of years. It is rather mind-bending that the National Space Centre's educational presentations explain that as we study many of the pinpoints of light in the sky, we are not seeing signs of the future as the Romans believed, but we are looking deep into the past. The light we see may have taken millions of years to reach us.

Welcome to Leicester

The biggest city in the East Midlands, Leicester is a fascinating and vibrant place with a long history. It's one of the oldest cities in Britain with evidence of a Celtic Iron Age settlement on the banks of the River Soar before the Romans arrived in AD 47 and built a substantial fort to defend their territory south of the Fosse Way. They called it *Ratae Coritanorum* meaning the ramparts of the Coritani tribe. The remains of the baths they built can be seen at the 'Jewry Wall Museum' that displays the ancient stonework and explains the importance of Leicester during the Roman occupation. The Romans built a protective wall around Leicester, and after the Norman invasion a motte and bailey fort was constructed on the same site with the town walls reinforced. But in medieval times the fortress fell into disrepair and Richard III refused to stay in the damp and cold castle before the battle of Bosworth Field in 1485, preferring the cosier Blue Boar pub.

Leicester Cathedral that dominates the centre of the city with its 220 foot spire was built on the site of a Roman temple and was dedicated to St. Martin of Tours, a 4th Century Roman officer who became a bishop. The original parts of the cathedral are 12th century, but most of it is Victorian with an imposing nave featuring sweeping arches along the sides. And in recent years there have been more than 100,000 visitors to the cathedral, most of them there to look at a block of pale Swaledale stone with a carved cross, mounted on a dark plinth of limestone. Beneath it in a brick-lined vault is an oak coffin containing the remains of King Richard III. The remarkable story of the discovery of his remains and his reburial in the cathedral attracted worldwide attention, and has given Leicester's tourism economy a significant boost.

Looking for Richard

The Leicester Richard III boom was mainly the result of the persistence, some might say the obsession, of an amateur historian and writer called Philippa Langley. She may also have been possessed of a sixth sense! She thought that King Richard III had suffered from a bad Tudor press, particularly from Shakespeare's striking characterisation of the monarch as a ruthless, deformed hunchback, and while researching Richard's life, she began to wonder if she could find his grave. It was known that after the Battle of Bosworth in 1485, the deposed king's body had been brought back to Leicester and was buried by The Grey Friars, a Franciscan holy order. There was a local story that at the time of the Reformation his bones had been dug up and and thrown into the River Soar by a mob. There is even a large stone plaque near the local Bow Bridge commemorating this story. But was it true? No one was quite sure where the old Grey Friars church would have stood, but Philippa managed to persuade the University of Leicester Archeological Services, the City Council and the Richard III Society that it would be worthwhile investigating the north end of the social services car park at 'Greyfriars'.

Philippa had visited Leicester in 2004, researching an intended book on Richard III, and she recounts that as she wandered into the car park and into the second parking bay, "I just felt I was walking on his grave. I can't explain it". A year later she returned and the feeling returned. But this time the letter 'R' had been painted on the same bay to mark it as reserved. For the researcher it was a sign. R for Richard. R for Rex. She was galvanised into action, and when the University of Leicester and the local authorities faltered in their commitment to a dig, she used crowdfunding to raise the additional finance required, pitched a programme idea to

Channel 4, and with considerable support from the Richard III Society, raised the £34,000 required. In August 2012, the car park was sealed off for two weeks, and the dig began. The archeologists wanted to find the remains of the medieval priory; most were deeply skeptical about finding Richard's remains.

On the first day of the dig, after just six hours, a skeleton was unearthed under the parking bay marked with an 'R'. It had battle wounds and a curved spine. Carbon-dating later established that the bones were from 1455-1540, coinciding with Richard's death in 1485. And more importantly, DNA sampling that the university had famously pioneered, matched the remains with known descendants of the last Plantagenet king. Beyond doubt, this was indeed the former monarch, the last English king to die in battle. Analysis of the bones established that he had suffered from scoliosis, affecting his spine, but he was not Shakespeare's hunchback with a deformed arm. The discovery had a huge impact locally, and also attracted attention around the world.

In March 2015, Richard III was reburied in Leicester Cathedral in the specially designed stone tomb in an elaborate ceremony. Thousands had lined the route, some throwing flowers, as his coffin in a smart modern hearse progressed through the streets of Leicester. Now, between the 700-year-old Leicester Market and the cathedral, you will find the 'King Richard III Visitor Centre', with interactive exhibits on his life, death, and grave discovery. Outside is a magnificent bronze statue of Richard looking heroic, with the crown in one hand and an enormous sword in the other. The Visitor Centre stands on the site of the medieval priory of the Grey Friars, and through a glass panel in the floor you can see an image of the king's skeleton that had lain there for 500 years. In 2013 the Channel 4 documentary was aired to great acclaim, and in

2015 Langley was awarded the MBE for her efforts, along with her colleague on the project John Ashdown-Hill. In 2022 Philippa Langley was portrayed by Sally Hawkins in 'The Lost King', a feature film directed by Stephen Frears. It took $4.5 million at the box office.

Meet Me at the Clock Tower

The centre of Leicester is a thriving shopping area with a large pedestrianised zone around the magnificent 70-foot high clock tower standing at the very centre of the city where five main thoroughfares meet. In early Victorian times, this central junction had become a bit of a nightmare, constantly jammed with horse-drawn vehicles jostling for space. So some shops were demolished to make more space, and the tower was erected in 1868, in effect becoming Britain's first traffic island or roundabout, though it took a few years before it was agreed that the horses, carts and carriages should all go round the clock in a clockwise direction. It has become Leicester's traditional meeting place. In fact it is more than a clock.

The 'Haymarket Memorial Clock Tower' was designed as a tribute to four of the city's most famous benefactors. They are commemorated at the four corners by Portland stone statues, finely carved by a local monumental mason, Samuel Barfield. Gazing down on the shoppers with extremely grave expressions, are Sir Thomas White, William Wigston, Alderman Gabriel Newton, and leaning casually on his sword - Simon de Montfort. White was a successful cloth merchant who used his immense wealth to establish schools and colleges, including St. John's College, Oxford, and the Merchant Taylor's School in London. I can't help wishing that the billionaires of today would use their loot to improve the lot of others rather than spend it on jets, yachts, mansions and rockets.

William Wigston, (actually 'Wiggeston' in the sixteenth century), was another benefactor who established almshouses and schools. And Gabriel Newton was an eighteenth century wool-comber and inn-keeper who must have been a bit of a charmer; he was married three times, each time to a very wealthy woman. He had no surviving children and left his fortune to the city to establish a charity school. As for Simon de Montfort, the 6th Earl of Leicester and brother-in-law of King Edward III, he famously led the Barons' Rebellion against the king in 1264 and ruled in the king's name for nearly a year before his defeat and death at the Battle of Evesham. De Montfort is credited with holding the first parliaments of representatives from around the country. Less celebrated is his violent antisemitism. He expelled or had murdered thousands of Jews in Leicester, Derby, Worcester and London.

Daniel Lambert doesn't have a statue on the clock tower, though he's probably better known locally than some of those commemorated. You can learn about this famous son of Leicester at the Newarke Houses social history museum. He became a national celebrity in the early 1800s. He claimed that he didn't eat or drink excessively, but from his teenage years he grew and grew until he weighed more than 50 stones. He became an attraction as 'The Fattest Man in England', and went to London in a specially constructed carriage to exploit his fame, charging a shilling for an audience. He was an articulate raconteur and gained a strong following among the society ladies in London. Even King George III requested an audience. During a lucrative nationwide tour, Daniel Lambert died while staying at the Waggon and Horses Inn in Stamford, having reached a weight of 52 stones 11 pounds and the age of 39. But how to remove his body? According to the Stamford Civic Chronicle, 20 men were engaged to remove a window, knock down a wall, and convey his huge coffin to the churchyard and a very large grave.

Multi-cultural Leicester

Woollen cloth made Leicester affluent. Quality clothing has been the city's speciality for centuries, and even today, there are plenty of clothes shops in the centre, including independent designer shops and all the main retail chains. At the top of High Street is Jubilee Square – an open space that was the site of the Roman forum and later the medieval marketplace where bolts of cloth would be traded and taken around the country. It flourished as a wool town in the Middle Ages, and in more recent years has retained its textile traditions - one reason why it is such a multi-cultural city. As the demand for quality clothing increased after the war, skilled seamstresses and knitters were encouraged to come from the Asian sub-continent, along with others who were willing to work in the newly mechanised factories for relatively low wages.

In 1972, Idi Amin announced that the entire Asian community in Uganda had 90 days to leave the country. About 6,000 of them settled in Leicester, despite the city council posting large adverts in the Uganda Argus newspaper telling Asian readers, 'Do not come to Leicester'. The city councillors were afraid their social services would be overwhelmed. That did not turn out to be the case, with many of the Ugandan Asians from educated families bringing with them skills and an entrepreneurial spirit which helped the city to flourish. Now Leicester celebrates its extraordinary diversity.

According to the 2021 census, 43.3% identify themselves as Asian or British Asian, 40.9% identify as white, 11.6% identify as black, black-British, Caribbean, African or of mixed ethnic groups, with 4.1% saying they are 'other'. The City Mayor, Sir Peter Soulsby, says, "I am very pleased and proud of our city of Leicester. It gets enormous praise for the diversity of its communities who contribute so much to every aspect of our lives." And Riaz Ravat, from the St. Philip's Centre that runs interfaith schemes, says, "The city is a beacon of hope on diversity because global communities have contributed richly to the social, economic and civic mosaic which makes up Leicester. People around the world have visited the city to understand our story."

The Fosse Way leading out of Leicester towards the south-west is called Narborough Road. In 2016 after a research project led by the London School of Economics into multi-cultural streets in the UK, Narborough Road was declared the most diverse street in Britain, and possibly the world. Shopkeepers along its straight mile-and-a-half had come from a total of 23 countries of birth. Certainly the bright colours of the clothes shops, the smells of spices and incense, the music, restaurants and food outlets make it extraordinarily vibrant and dynamic, especially in the autumn when, along with the Fosse Way on the other side of the city where it is called Belgrave Road, the Diwali festival of lights attracts thousands of visitors. It is thought to be the biggest celebration of the Hindu festival outside India. It's strange to think that back in 1485, Richard III rode out of Leicester down Narborough Road to meet his doom at Bosworth Field, with thousands of people cheering him on his way. There would have been no cheering when Henry Tudor's men returned up the Fosse Way with Richard's naked body slung over a horse – not the kind of steed he had been calling for, according to Shakespeare, when surrounded at Bosworth.

Voles, Coconuts, and Eau de Mink

Still inside the ring road to the left of Narborough Road is an urban oasis - the Aylestone Meadows Local Nature Reserve.

It's a large area of peaceful greenspace between the rivers Soar and Biam, with several locks along the Grand Union Canal that links London with the Midlands. The wetland, the meadows and ribbons of woodland, are criss-crossed by well-maintained paths and boardwalks, so it's easy to see some of the wide variety of wildlife close to the city centre. There is even an outside chance you might glimpse the rare water vole, or hear a plop as one drops into the canal, because just a couple of miles down the Grand Union, the Wildlife Trusts and Canal and River Trust have started a long-term project to make the banks more water vole friendly, and to trap the voracious feral mink that have devastated the vole population across England. And surprisingly the little voles are being helped out by coconuts.

Once widespread in England, water voles, whose most famous incarnation is Ratty in *The Wind in the Willows*, have suffered a 90% drop in numbers in the last fifty years, making it the fastest declining mammal in the country. The female mink is small enough to get into their nest holes and eat the young. Mink can even scale steep banks and devastate sand martin colonies. In some parts of the country there have been water vole reintroduction programmes, but many conservationists reckon there isn't much point in reintroducing voles if the causes for the decline aren't removed. So that means getting rid of the mink, and creating banks on canals and rivers where there is the right kind of habitat for nesting and feeding. Three-metre long coir roll mats made from coconut husks, are being installed, along with a variety of aquatic plants. They'll provide food and shelter, allowing the voles to burrow into the bank and make their homes away from predators. Local ecologist Chloe Walker says, "We are installing the coir rolls, which are essentially long rolls of planting material, along the hard-edged canal banks to create an instant habitat. I think water voles are just the most charming little animals. If you've ever been lucky enough to see them interacting in their normal habitat, munching away on the vegetation, there's just something magical about them you can't really quite describe."

As for the mink, a scent lure obtained from the anal glands of trapped mink is now proving to be irresistible to the animals. Charmingly called 'Eau de Mink', the lure is being used in cages to entice and trap the animals. According to the Waterlife Recovery Trust, a trial in East Anglia using the scent lure has eliminated mink in one region leading to a recovery in the species on which it preys. They claim, somewhat optimistically in my view, that if this method of trapping is widely used, the whole of Britain could be cleared of mink in five years.

Fosse Meadows

Leaving Leicester on the B4114, we fork left on to the B4455 'Old Roman Road' that follows the straight route all the way to Shipston on Stour where it will join the A429. To the right of the road is another valuable wildlife area - the Fosse Meadows Country Park, managed by Blaby District Council. It's a hundred acres of mixed habitats – meadows, a plantation, a lake with a bird hide, and an area of broadleaf woodland, which to my mind could do with some thinning out, as the understorey, or scrub layer as it is known, is rather bare in places. But with free car parks, toilets and picnic areas, it's a very popular venue with a pleasant walk beside a meandering brook that feeds the River Soar. The banks are visual symphony of yellows and greens, with the weeping willows covered in curly catkins, and clumps of marsh marigolds with petals like polished metal. If you fancy a pub lunch, you can wander along to nearby Sharnford and 'The Bricklayers' or 'The Sharnford Arms', or to 'The Pig in Muck' that brews its own beer in the attractive village of Claybrooke Magna. The 18th century watermill there is still operating, and produces about 40 different varieties of flour, including spicy tomato mix and chilli mix, which give hot-buttered toast a different meaning.

There has been yet more rain and the ground is saturated. There has been no serious snow in the midlands all winter, and not many frosts. The predictions from scientists that climate warming will mean climate wetting for the UK appear to be coming true, with more flooding, more winter storms, but drier, hotter summers. The World Meteorological Organisation has just issued its latest report called 'Red Alert to the World'. It confirmed that the previous year was the hottest on record, with some records 'smashed', including sea temperatures, the rise in sea levels, the loss of polar ice and glacier retreat.

Here in the East Midlands it is unusually mild and spring is certainly springing in mid-March. The country park is alive with birdsong with the sharp repetitive phrases of the song thrushes contrasting with the relaxed fluting of the blackbirds. And there are chiffchaffs calling their name from the willows by the lake. These fragile warblers may be early arrivals from southern Europe or North Africa, but many will have stayed in England throughout the winter. According to the British Trust for Ornithology, increasing numbers of chiffchaffs are staying all year as the climate warms and insects can be found even in the depths of winter. Its relative, the willow warbler, is almost identical. If you can get a really close view, the chiffchaff has black legs and the willow warbler has flesh-coloured legs. But spotting the leg-colour of these tiny birds is incredibly difficult. So the best means of identification is to listen to their contrasting songs; the willow warbler has a delicate cascading song, very different from the loud 'chiff-chaff' of its identical cousin.

They also have very different behaviours. The willow warblers that will soon be arriving in Britain are long-distance migrants from southern Africa, and are capable of extraordinary journeys for a bird weighing just 9 grams. With geo-location tracking, individuals have been followed from Mozambique to North East Russia and back again, a round trip of eighteen thousand miles. These little warblers are unusual in that they moult twice a year to ensure their flight feathers are in tip-top condition before the epic journeys in spring and autumn.

High Cross

The A4114 deviates slightly from the original route to pass through the village of Sharnforth, and for 2 miles the Fosse Way itself is followed by a minor road, called, unsurprisingly, 'Roman Road'. It's a single track lane running over a slightly domed strip of land with deep ditches on either side that were dug 2,000 years ago during the construction of the *agger*. There's a constant hum of traffic now, with the M69 to the right, and ahead the Fosse Way crosses the busy A5 at 'High Cross'. For two thousand years this has been an important crossroads, for the A5 follows the route of another of the great Roman roads - Watling Street. In fact, like the Fosse Way, this straight road was almost certainly created by the Ancient Britons, and later paved by the Romans to permit the rapid deployment of troops and supplies in all weathers. It ran for 276 miles from Dover, through London fording the Thames at Westminster, to St. Albans and on to North Wales. Here at the intersection of the two great roads, the Romans constructed a fort called *Venonis*. It represents the centre of Roman Britain.

The existence of the fort came to light in 1968 when an RAF veteran called Kenneth St. Joseph was flying over in a Cessna Skymaster and saw the traces of a complex of buildings in a field near the junction. During the war he had served as an Intelligence Analyst looking at photos of bombing targets, and being interested in history, he thought aerial photography could help to uncover sites of archeological significance. He's now regarded as the pioneer of archeology from the air, and was to become Professor of Aerial Photographic Studies at Cambridge University. In the past sixty years, thousands of ancient sites across the UK have been revealed by aerial photography, some dating back to the stone age.

In medieval times, there was a gibbet at High Cross, where the bodies of felons might be left to hang for months, to deter robber-gangs and highwaymen who operated along the turnpikes. In 1722, the Earl of Denbigh replaced the wooden gibbet with a tall stone monument, apparently to mark the Duke of Blenheim's victories against France. Quite why he thought this was good idea is not clear to me. But in 1791, a bolt of lightning shattered the stone spike, and today all that is left is a 15-foot base, looking rather forlorn. In Roman times, this intersection of the two big roads protecting their British empire might well have been the location of one of the most significant, and bloodiest battles between the invading legions and the Celtic tribes. Known as 'The Defeat of Boudica' or 'The Battle of Watling Street', it took place in about AD 60; historians aren't quite sure which year it was, or indeed exactly where it took place - but somewhere near High Cross is a decent bet.

According to Tacitus, the massed armies of the Iceni led by Queen Boudica, and other tribes who opposed the occupiers, had marched on *Londonium* (London), razed it to the ground, then turned their attention to *Verulamium* (St. Albans) further north along Watling Street. The Roman General Suetonius had assembled legions from across occupied England, and ten thousand elite troops intercepted the rebel tribes somewhere near Rugby, and it's likely he would have used the newly paved Fosse Way to bring them in rapidly from east and west.

The resulting battle was a massacre of the Britons. Tacitus says 80,000 were killed. Boudica committed suicide rather than be captured. The Roman occupation of southern England was secure and would remain so for nearly 400 years.

The A5 at the Fosse Way is the ancient boundary between Leicestershire and the territory of the powerful Earls of Warwick. So at the High Cross junction with Watling Street, we move into Shakespeare's county, Warwickshire.

April

The Heart of England

When proud-pied April, dressed in all his trim,
Hath put a spirit of youth in everything...
(Shakespeare's Sonnet No 98)

Sedge Warbler

Warwickshire

The Fosse Way followed by the modern B4455 shoots straight through Warwickshire, proclaimed on the road signs as 'Shakespeare's County'. It is named after the county town of Warwick that was founded in the tenth century by the formidable Aethelflaed, 'Lady of the Mercians'. The name Warwick comes from the Anglo-Saxon *Wer-wic* - the settlement by the weir. There is a natural shelf in the riverbed making the Avon fordable below the cliff where the Norman castle now stands. The Roman Road passes to the east of Coventry, Leamington Spa, Warwick, and Shakespeare's Stratford-upon-Avon before entering the Cotswolds. First it passes a small village called Monks Kirby, population 250, with a magnificent parish church dedicated to St. Edith. She was the daughter of Edgar, a 10th century king of England. Monks Kirby has been inhabited since at least Roman times, with evidence, (Roman urns and bricks), found around the Church suggesting either a Roman cemetery or villa on the site.

Our route passes over the M6, Britain's longest motorway and one of the busiest. At any time of day or night there seem to be rivers of metal flowing in both directions. Just beyond the M6 is Stretton-under-Fosse, (Stretton means a settlement or town on the 'Street' – the Roman Road), and the pretty village of Brinklow. There's an unusual kink in the Fosse Way here, and archeologists have established that there was a pre-Roman burial mound near the present day church, and that the road-builders decided to go around it, perhaps from respect for the dead, but more likely from superstition that bad luck would ensue if they disturbed the Celtic graves. The Normans were less concerned about ancient ghosts, or Tolkien style 'barrow-wights', and built a motte-and-bailey fortification on the mound, called Brinklow Castle. It's now known locally by the less grandiose names of The Big Hill, or The Tump.

A mile further on is the hamlet of Bretford, with a gorgeous bridge over the River Avon. It dates from the thirteenth century, so the locals may have been building this stone bridge to replace a wooden footbridge around the time that King John was signing Magna Carta. In Old English Bretford means 'plank ford', indicating a wooden footbridge next to the ford. The stone bridge has been extensively renovated over the years, and is now wide enough to carry single-line traffic. Alongside is a concrete pedestrian walkway mounted on pillars well above the flood plain. Curiously this quiet place played a role in WWII. Just outside the village, a lighting decoy was set up in the fields – hundreds of lights designed to fool the Luftwaffe pilots into thinking they had found their targets, the armaments factories of Coventry. I'm afraid the ruse didn't work. The city was bombed relentlessly during the war. On November 14th 1940, a mass raid by more than 500 bombers plastered Coventry with incendiary bombs and high explosives, destroying most of the city centre including the medieval cathedral, and killing 568 people. There's no record of any bombs being dropped in the fields around Bretford.

Many of the buildings here are constructed of warm orange-red bricks, with the clay quarried from a belt of russet triassic 'mudstone, siltstone and sandstone'. Warwickshire sandstone isn't particularly strong, so many of the stone walls along our route show signs of repair after crumbling. To the south-east of the Fosse Way, the bedrock is a grey lias limestone of higher quality, as landowner Tom Walker discovered in 1825. With his son George, he opened a small quarry on his land at Newbold-on-Avon, three miles east of the Fosse Way, and began producing lime mortar. The mortar was soon popular with local builders, so the father and son founded a company and started producing Portland Cement. The nineteenth century building boom meant that concrete, a mixture of cement and sand, was in great demand and the business flourished. After many mergers and take-overs, Rugby Cement is now owned by a billionaire Mexican under the name 'Cemex'. It employs 40,000 people worldwide and has an annual turnover of £12 billion. Tom and George would be proud.

A Superb Nature Reserve

A short diversion through the village of Brandon takes us to the best nature reserve in the county, the headquarters of the Warwickshire Wildlife Trust, Brandon Marsh. It's a surprisingly large area so close to the centre of Coventry – 230 acres in fact. The reserve is based on former gravel pits and cement works, and is now a mixture of pools, fen, scrubland and large reed beds, with the Warwickshire Avon meandering through. Throughout the year it is rich in bird life, insects, fungi, and flora, with seven hides overlooking the pools. In winter the sounds above the hissing of the reeds are of honking geese or whistling ducks, or the rushing wings of starlings arriving in their tens of thousands on cold evenings for spectacular murmurations, before pouring into the reed beds to roost. In April the sounds of the wildfowl have been replaced by a cacophony of bird song from the thickets and woodland, and black-headed gulls and common terns are screaming overhead as they compete for prime nest sites on the sandy islands.

The terns have just arrived from their winter territories in Northern Spain and the west coast of Africa. They are gorgeous birds with blood red bills and forked tails that have given them the nickname of 'sea swallows'. They are agile in flight and plunge into the water to catch fish. Also preparing to nest on the islands in the Brandon Marsh pools are black and white oystercatchers with their bright orange bills. Their noisy piping reminds me of summer holidays by the sea; but in the last 50 years, oystercatchers have increasingly moved inland to breed, changing their diet from shellfish in the rock-pools to worms found on open fields. Perhaps they became fed up with coastal pollution and the increasing number of violent storms around our coasts.

Little Brown Birds

Brandon Marsh shows many signs of the warming climate. Across the reserve the explosive call of the Cetti's warbler can be heard in the spring. This little brown bird, named after the 18th century Italian zoologist Francesco Cetti who identified it, was first recorded in Britain in 1961. It doesn't migrate south like most other warblers, so is vulnerable to harsh winters here. But as the winter months in southern and central England have become more benign, this little warbler is spreading north rapidly. Also as I walk along the wooded paths of Brandon Marsh I can hear the song of another plain brown warbler - the garden warbler. It has a gorgeous rippling song, not unlike that of its cousin the blackcap, but richer and softer.

All across the reserve, two more brown warblers are in full song. The reed warbler lives up to its name and sticks to the reed beds, emitting a scratchy repetitive call. The song of the sedge warbler can be confused with it because of some similar repeated notes, but to my mind the little sedge warbler is much more creative, mimicking other birds in a continuous stream of squeaking, babbling and chattering, often from an exposed perch. The sedge warbler is pretty easy to identify if you catch sight of one; it has a cream stripe over the eye, called a supercilium, and a dark cap giving it a stripy-headed look. The pioneer naturalist Rev. Gilbert White was the first to distinguish these two warblers, noting the 'creamy white eyebrow' of the sedge warbler. The poet Edward Thomas was particularly fond of the song of the sedge warbler, and in 1915, the year he volunteered for WWI, only to be killed in the trenches at Arras, he paused on a country walk to write:

> ... *And sedge-warblers, clinging so light*
> *To willow-twigs, sang longer than the lark,*
> *Quick, shrill or grating, a song to match the heat*
> *Of the strong sun, nor less the water's cool,*
> *Gushing through narrows, swirling in the pool.*

Certainly I think that the gorgeous sound of a sedge warbler at full throttle is one of the classic sounds of an English riverbank in the spring.

More evidence of our warming climate are the little egrets and great white egrets that are now regulars on the Brandon Marsh reserve, after expanding their northern ranges rapidly in recent years. And now they are being followed by cattle egrets, once only seen on the backs of buffalo in Africa or cattle in southern Europe, but in the last few years breeding successfully in south-west England and East Anglia. Cattle egrets were seen for the first time at Brandon Marsh in 2020, and in 2023 one turned up in a paddock on the north side of Warwick; it's just a matter of time before they breed at Brandon Marsh. A total of 237 bird species have been recorded at the reserve since 1981, when the French cement company Lafarge agreed to lease the site to the Wildlife Trust for 99 years at a rent of just £1 per year. Merci!

The 'Immortal 29th Division'

South of Brandon, the B4455 Fosse Way crosses the A45 at a large roundabout with an intriguing white obelisk towering above the traffic. I've driven past it many times and wondered what this stone spike was commemorating. But there was nowhere nearby to park and walk back, and to cross on to the traffic island would have risked life and limb. So I looked it up online. This is what the plaque says:

> *'Here in the centre of England where Telford's coaching road from London to Holyhead is crossed by the Roman Fosse Way, on the 12th of March 1915, His Majesty King George V reviewed his troops of the immortal XXIX Division shortly before they embarked for active service in Gallipoli. In memory of their stay in Warwickshire 1914-15 and their incomparable services since.'*

So there we are. The 29th Division, known as the Incomparable Division as well as 'The Immortals', was a famous infantry unit that fought throughout the disastrous Gallipoli Campaign, including at the original landing on Cape Helles. Then from 1916 to the end of the WWI the division fought on the Western Front in Belgium and France.

It's recorded in the regimental records that 'The total casualties of the 29th Division amounted to something like 94,000. Gallipoli alone accounted for 34,000. This must be among the highest totals in any division. … The number of Victoria Crosses won by members of this division was 27, (12 at Gallipoli). This constitutes a record. A large commemorative Portland Stone obelisk, built in 1921 to remember the Division's review by King George V before they were sent to Gallipoli, is located on a roundabout on the A45 just north of Stretton-on-Dunsmore, Warwickshire'. Apparently the memorial was originally flanked by captured German guns, but these were removed during the Second World War.

The Feldon and the Forest

The 16th century poet and local history writer, John Leland, wrote that Warwickshire was divided into two landscapes on either side of the valley of the River Avon that meanders south-west until it joins the Severn at Tewkesbury. To the south is the 'Feldon', essentially rich agricultural land, partly on the flood plains of the Avon and the Stour, and to the north was the 'Forest of Arden', well known to Shakespeare because his ancestors had farmed in clearings in the forest. Since that time, a lot more of the old forest has been cleared, but there are still some ancient woodlands remaining, and plenty of patches of wetland along the Avon valley, all keenly protected by environmental charities.

The reserves near this section of the Fosse Way are immensely valuable to the large urban populations of Coventry, (population 350,000, making it the 10th largest city in the UK), Leamington Spa and Daventry. Popular among the nearby urban-dwellers are Ryton Pools, just to the west of the Fosse Way, and the connected Bubbenhall Wood. The hundred-acre Ryton Pools Country Park is run by the County Council, and has excellent disabled access to a couple of hides overlooking the pools and paths around the meadows, scrubland and ribbons of woodland. The adjoining Bubbenhall Wood, managed by the Warwickshire Wildlife Trust, has been here a long time. It's mentioned in the Domesday Book of 1086, listed as 2 furlongs long and two furlongs wide, (about the size of 12 football pitches). There are plans to link up the woods with nearby copses and hedgerows to establish some wildlife corridors - vitally important for our natural diversity. At the Ryton reserve in April the brown and white sand martins have arrived, hawking athletically for insects across the pools, the great spotted woodpeckers are drumming in the woods, and their larger cousins the green woodpeckers are 'yaffling' from the rough ground where they are probing for ants in the grassy tussocks and mole hills.

Witches' Thimbles

And a stone's throw away is the Wappenbury Wood reserve, also managed by the Warwickshire Wildlife Trust, with their dedicated volunteers giving up their time to preserve the irreplaceable habitat. This is another truly old wood. The Domesday Book says that Richard of Wappenbury was given 'rights' over the wood, probably for fuel, building materials and hunting. Now it is particularly rich in plants, birds and butterflies, with grassy rides, glades and a waymarked trail. At this time of year it is awash with the smokey azure hue of bluebells. They spend most of the year as bulbs underground in ancient woodland, only emerging to flower and leaf from April onwards. This early flowering allows them to make the most of the sunlight that's still able to reach the forest floor before the tree canopy becomes too dense.

These are British or English bluebells, not to be confused with the Spanish bluebells that were introduced into Victorian gardens and are spreading in England as they tend to out-compete the native species. The British bluebells found in ancient woods are a dark violet-blue, and the flowers grow on one side of the stem, so that they droop. The slightly paler Spanish bluebell has flowers around the stem and stands straighter and taller, and it doesn't have the familiar sweet scent of the native flower. The sticky sap of the bluebell was once used to bind the pages of books and glue the feathers onto arrows, and during the Elizabethan period, the bulbs were crushed to make starch for the ruffs of collars and cuffs. So Shakespeare may have been wearing bluebell starch when he wrote of the flowers in Cymbeline, though he called them 'azured hare-bells'; the names bluebell and harebell were interchangeable in those days. There's plenty of folklore surrounding these lovely flowers, often involving witches and fairies. In various parts of the country they are known as *witches' thimbles, dead man's bells*, or north of the border, *aul' man's bells* – the old man in question being the Devil. It was said that the ringing of the bluebells would summon the fairies to their gatherings. And don't ever pick a bluebell, or you will be led away by the fairy folk, never to be seen again.

Victorian Boom Town

Three miles to the right of the Fosse Way is Royal Leamington Spa, awarded the regal title in 1838 by Queen Victoria who had visited the town a few years earlier as a princess, and had become a big fan of the health properties of the salty spring water. She returned to the spa in 1848, and her patronage helped to make Leamington the fastest growing town in Britain. In the census of 1801, the population was recorded as 315. The census of 1901, (incidentally the year of Victoria' death), recorded the population as nearly 27,000. There is a fine statue of the monarch near the entrance to the attractive Jephson Gardens along the banks of the River Leam at the bottom of the main shopping street, The Parade. Her expression looks like she has just taken a sip of the foul-tasting spa water. Leamington is a very good centre for shopping, but like other town centres, has been somewhat affected by the development of a big shopping retail park on the outskirts. These days the town has developed as the UK's major centre for producing video games, gaining it the nickname, 'Silicon Spa'. It has also become a major regional centre for fine art, design and music. There's no cathedral here to attract nesting peregrines, but that hasn't deterred the falcons. With encouragement from the District Council and the local Wildlife Trust, they have nested for many years in a gravel-filled tray in the clock tower at the top of the town hall, successfully raising chicks each year. With webcams following their progress, they have become a much admired local attraction. At the moment the falcons are taking it turns to brood four reddish-brown eggs.

Beyond Leamington, the Fosse Way crosses the UK's longest canal, the Grand Union. It came into being in 1929 with the amalgamation of the Regents Canal in London, the Grand Junction Canal at Brentford, and the Warwick Canals. It shortened the time barges could travel between the capital and the industrial midlands, and a number of the locks were widened to accommodate bigger vessels or two narrowboats side-by-side, all to try, somewhat desperately in hindsight, to remain competitive with the expanding rail and road networks. The canal companies were fighting a losing battle. After the Second World War, commercial traffic ended on the Grand Union, and many of the country's canals fell into disrepair. But with the help of thousands of volunteers, many working with the Canal and River Trust, Britain's canal network has found a new life as a much enjoyed leisure facility for narrow-boaters, anglers and walkers.

Boats and Trains

Suddenly we are crossing another major piece of engineering designed to speed up the journey from London to Birmingham. On either side of the Fosse Way there are wide scars across the fields, plastic fencing galore, mobile toilets and huge earth-moving machines. This is the route of HS2. The controversial High Speed Two rail project began in 2009 when the HS2 Ltd company was formed, and feasibility studies were presented to the government. The original vision was for a new line to connect London Euston with Birmingham, Manchester, Leeds, the East Midlands and ultimately Scotland, with services reaching speeds of up to 225 MPH, and creating greater capacity, particularly on the badly overcrowded West Coast Main Line. In London it would link with Crossrail to allow travellers from the north a rapid onward journey in the capital. It would help to 'level-up' the north and south of the UK. The estimated cost in 2009 was £37.5 billion. I was quite enthusiastic about the idea, envious of the fabulous high speed trains in France, Spain and Germany. Unfortunately HS2 has turned into an embarrassing and expensive shambles.

There have been countless arguments about the precise route; the amount of tunnelling required in built-up areas was seriously underestimated. Assumptions of the impact of inflation were extremely optimistic, with delays designed to 'save money' doing the opposite. The compensation fund for affected properties was inadequate. Plans for a hub at Crewe were soon dropped. There were many challenges in the courts requiring judicial review, notably from environmental groups about HS2's impact assessments on nature. After a lot of work on the site, Euston proved to be physically impossible and far too expensive to accommodate a new high speed London terminal. Ten years on from the initial launch of HS2, the overall cost estimate from the Department of Transport had risen to a staggering £98 billion. In 2021, the government cancelled the leg to the East Midlands and Leeds, and at the Conservative Party Conference in 2022, held in Manchester incidentally, Rishi Sunak announced that the entire northern leg was to be cancelled, dismaying the mayors of northern cities.

The Phase One section that remained would end at Old Oak Common station in West London. In 2023 its estimated cost was put at around £55 billion, but it seems to me the only benefit would be to expand passenger capacity between London and Birmingham when it finally opens sometime in the 2030s, though we don't know how expensive the tickets might be, or how popular the new service might be. Under current plans, passengers planning to use the high-speed route would have to get to Curzon Street in Birmingham or Acton in West London, seven miles from Euston. As you can tell, I am very disillusioned about the way HS2 has been mismanaged. As I write, a group of northern mayors are trying to revive the legs beyond Birmingham with private investment covering the enormous costs. I wish them luck.

But as an environmentalist I find the destruction of valuable wild habitats in the centre of England upsetting. The Wildlife Trusts issued a special report called, 'What's the Damage?', cataloguing the habitats affected directly by the construction. And in 2023 the Trusts issued a new report focussing on 'How the UK's largest infrastructure project undervalued nature and overvalued its compensation measures'. It says, 'They got their figures hugely wrong'. According to a coalition of environmental charities, half of natural habitats could be lost along the route of HS2 between London and the West Midlands. The Woodland Trust estimated that 55 ancient woodlands would be impacted along this Phase One route. The coalition of environmental groups accused the government-owned company of using an accounting tool that was 'untested, out of date and fundamentally flawed' to assess its impact on nature. It claimed that along the route there will be 'at least 17% less nature present' after construction of Phase One between London and Birmingham - whereas HS2 Ltd says 'there will only be a 2.6% nature loss.' That's quite a difference. HS2 Ltd has committed a lot of money to planting trees after the construction work, but young trees can't really replace the deep ecosystems of the ancient forests and flower meadows - at least not for many generations.

Two thousand years ago, the Romans had no problems with judicial reviews or online campaigns to delay the construction of the Fosse Way. From here the route they made in a handful of years drives pencil-straight past the outskirts of Leamington and towards the Cotswolds.

May

Warwickshire to the Cotswolds

Choirs of songbirds greet each day
With eulogies, as if to say:
'Whosoever plants a tree
Winks at immortality!'
(Felix Dennis)

Man Orchid

Spring Flowers

Our route south from Leamington passes beside another nature reserve based on the extraction of limestone from the line of lias rock across central England. The Ufton Fields wildlife reserve is unusual in that the quarrying left ridges of spoil with flooded areas in between, creating strips of different habitats. Plants thrive on the lime rich soil; the rare 'man orchid' can be found here, with amazing flowers that look remarkably like human forms with four limbs, staring eyes, and generously endowed male genitalia. The Midlands is at the extreme north of the range of this warm-weather orchid. Ufton Fields is also important for other wildflowers, fungi, butterflies, birds and a variety of water life including toads, newts, and dragonflies. In May it is buzzing with insects gathering the sweet pollen from the foxgloves, dog roses, purple loosestrife, cow parsley and yellow rattle that splash white, yellow and mauve across the fields. The weather has improved at last after a dreadfully wet winter, and the colours of the blossom and spring flowers are vibrant under bright blue skies.

But elsewhere in the world there is plenty of evidence of the weather extremes and climate disruption that is happening more often. South Asia is like a furnace with record high temperatures across Thailand, Mayanmar, Vietnam, Bangladesh and parts of India. Dozens of people have died from heatstroke and schools are closed. Latin America is enduring record temperatures. In China's most populous province, Guangdong, over 100,000 people have been evacuated from their homes after massive floods overwhelmed towns and cities, and in the UAE the authorities are mopping up after Dubai was completely flooded with a year's rainfall in two days. Climate change is going to be a huge challenge in years to come.

A mile further on down the Fosse, with pale yellow cowslips embroidering the grass verges, is Harbury, an unassuming village that has a long history. The village is on a hill 400ft above sea level – a strategic and defensible location; there are remains of a hill fort from iron age times here. The name of the village derives from Hereburgh's Byrig - 'byrig' being an Anglo-Saxon term meaning a fortified village or settlement. Hereburgh (or Heber) is thought to have been the female leader of an Iron Age tribe who settled at the site about five hundred years before the Roman invasion. The Romans built a fort at nearby Chesterton, a hill that is now topped by one of Warwickshire's most famous landmarks, the Chesterton Windmill.

Wind Power

It is a beautiful and striking structure, built by the Lord of the Manor, Sir Edward Peyto, in the early 1630s, and renovated several times since. It has a cylindrical milling area raised about fifteen feet above the ground on six brick pillars, presumably designed in its elevated position to keep out rats and mice. The sails have been replaced several times in the past 500 years, the latest time being in 2006. It was an open day and one of the visitors was standing admiring the old mill when one of the sails fell off and hit him. He was injured, but not too badly. The mill had to be sealed off until all the sails had been strengthened. You can visit it on open days in the summer, and see the oldest working parts of a 'tower mill' in the country.

Interestingly, in Newport Rhode Island in the USA, there is a similar mill built on stone towers. It's known that it was built by Benedict Arnold in about 1676, a hundred years before America's independence. So why is it similar to the Warwickshire windmill? It seems the Arnold family had migrated to America in 1635 from Leamington Priors, as the original Leamington hamlet was known, and from a village further down the Fosse Way near Ilchester. Benedict rose to become governor of Rhode Island. It's generally accepted now that the old mill on Rhode Island is based on the Chesterton Windmill, and it is much venerated as one of the oldest structures in the state.

The Windhover

It is open country here with wide fields of grass, barley and wheat, and as we pass over the M40 motorway, riding the breezes that drove the sails of the windmill is a kestrel, hovering with its head pointing into the wind like a weathervane, tail twitching to keep it steady. The male has a slate grey head and tail; the tail of the larger female is richly patterned in rows of spots. This lovely little falcon has benefitted from the expansion of the road networks. It is often seen hunting along the roadside verges where the rough banks with few humans wandering about are rich in voles, the kestrel's staple food. I also have a theory that the constant movement and noise of the traffic makes it easier for the kestrels to hover over the verge unnoticed. They are supposed to be 'crepuscular', meaning mainly active at dawn and dusk, but in my experience you can see them at any time of day, particularly in May when they will be feeding a brood of hungry youngsters.

I have a particular affection for kestrels, not only because they are so attractive and clearly beneficial to farmers, but because the 'windhover', as countryfolk would call this gingery bird of prey, encouraged my own interest in birds and wildlife. When I was a small boy at school, I would often be admonished for staring out of the window. But there was a drama going on out there. Next to the playing field was a large rubbish dump, and I would be watching the kestrel quartering the area systematically, then dropping, hovering, dropping, hovering, and then plunging in, sometimes wheeling away with a mouse or a young rat in its talons, the dangling tail visible. "Sorry, sir. I was watching a bird catching a rat."

Stand and Deliver

The roundabout at the junction of the Fosse Way and Harbury Lane, just north of the M40, is called Bendigo Mitchell Junction. So who was the interestingly-named Bendigo? In Warwickshire, his name is fairly well-known - perhaps not as familiar as that of Dick Turpin, but certainly with the same mixture of disapproval and admiration for highwaymen, as captured in the pop song 'Stand and Deliver' by Adam and the Ants. Eighteenth century records show that Bendigo Mitchell, (probably given the biblical name Abednego by Mr. and Mrs. Mitchell), was a feared highwayman who operated along the turnpikes of the Midlands, leading a gang of armed robbers based at The Trumpet Inn. The Fosse Way was his main base of operations. The authorities were determined to catch him and assembled a posse of armed volunteer constables to hunt him down.

On one occasion when cornered, he spurred his horse across the frozen Chesterton Mill ponds, with his pursuers reluctant to follow. His horse slipped and staggered but didn't fall, and gained the name 'Skater'. Bendigo became something of a romantic figure, stealing from the moneyed classes, though I don't think there is any record of him giving the loot to the poor! There's a large painting of the highwayman holding up a stage coach with a flintlock pistol in each hand and mounted on Skater, on the doorway of The Black Horse Inn in Warwick. It's just across the road from where he eventually met his doom. In 1776 he was captured by the sheriff's men and brought to trial at Warwick assizes. It is said his public hanging, (on an execution site that is now part of the Warwick Sainsbury's car park), was attended by 10,000 cheering spectators.

The highwayman's name lives on, not only on the name of a roundabout and at a local fork lift truck company called Bendigo Mitchell Ltd, but in a ballad written by the Warwickshire musicians, 'Wychwood Folk Rock', with the chorus:

> *And it's Hi Ho Skater Away*
> *I ride the Warwick Turnpike and the Old Fosse Way*
> *You'd best hold up your hands when I bid you to stand*
> *And it's Hey Ho Skater Away.*

Our way passes the ancient village of Moreton Morrell, the home of the agricultural training centre of Warwickshire College, with extensive grounds, an equine centre, and in recent years courses in sustainable farming methods that don't damage the environment. I think the students who will go on to put into action this kind of modern farming will be in the frontline of the battle to reverse biodiversity decline in Britain. There is no doubt at all that intensive farming in the past 70 years has caused great damage to nature. Insect numbers are down. Farmland birds such as yellowhammers and lapwings are in steep decline. Rivers have been polluted by run-off from fields treated with chemicals. Farming is tough, and in many areas it must be a struggle to make a decent living. But removing hedgerows and copses to expand fields, or using loads of insecticides on arable crops can lead to wildlife deserts. Moreton Morrell College is using science and best practice to encourage the next generation of farmers to preserve wild habitats, and there are now subsidies to help the development of sustainable farming, though the former Head of Agriculture at the college says many farmers believe the subsidies are inadequate and involve too much paperwork.

Compton Verney

Just a short distance down the Fosse Way we find the entrance to Compton Verney. The curved drive leads us to a classic 18th century English stately home set in 120 acres of parkland, with an interesting past and a very lively present. The grand house was built in 1714 for the family of the Baron Willoughby de Broke by the influential architect John Vanbrugh. It was remodelled by Robert Adam in the fashionable neoclassical style, while the grounds were redesigned by Lancelot 'Capability' Brown to appear more natural, with curves and vistas rather than straight rows of flower beds and regimented lines of trees. Brown damned a stream to create an attractive lake, allowing the approach to the house to cross a stone bridge with views in either direction, and with cedar trees reflected in the water. The succeeding generations found it difficult to maintain the large estate and the house changed hands several times. In 1921, it was bought by Joseph Watson, a soap manufacturer from Leeds who had made a fortune when he sold out to Unilever, and had decided to devote the rest of his life to horse racing and the life of a country gentleman. In 1922 he was made the 1st Baron Manton of Compton Verney for his wartime service providing munitions. Unfortunately the ennobled Joseph didn't have the chance to enjoy his new found status. A few weeks later, he had a fatal heart attack when riding with the Warwickshire Hunt. After WWII, when Compton Verney had been requisitioned by the army, it gradually fell into disrepair.

When I was a child, my father 'did the pools' each week. For readers too young to know, the football pools were a form of gambling that was hugely popular, well before the National Lottery, with Littlewoods, Vernons and Zetters posting out coupons to be filled-in and returned with a cheque, or given to an agent who would knock on the door and take the coupon. As I recall, my Dad would try to predict eight score-draws in the matches taking place the following weekend, (always kicking off at 3pm on a Saturday, before lucrative TV rights changed all that). At 5pm on the match day, we would tune our Roberts radio to the BBC Light Programme to hear the football results on 'Sports Report'. I would enter the scores into a table on the back page of the Daily Express while Dad sucked at his pipe. By the 1950s the Post Office was handling 15 million entries a week and the pools business employed 100,000 people to check each entry by hand.

Peter Moores had inherited the Littlewoods chain of shops, mail order companies and football pools business from his father, John, the son of a bricklayer and later founder of John Moores University in Liverpool. Peter became a collector of fine art and used his wealth to support theatre, opera, music and community arts projects. In 1993, he bought the semi-derelict Compton Verney, extending and refurbishing it to create a magnificent art gallery and a venue for contemporary theatrical and musical performances, and the grounds have a spectacular light show each Christmas. The galleries contain notable portraits of British Kings and Queens, Chinese bronzes, Neapolitan art and the national collection of British Folk Art, as well as special exhibitions each year. When I win the lottery and become filthy rich, I hope I will be inspired by the Moores family to invest in a similar way in education and culture that is accessible to all.

To the right along the A422 lies Stratford-upon-Avon, world famous because of the son of a glove-maker who went off to London to become the dazzling playwright of the Elizabethan era. These days the town is almost overwhelmed in the summer with tourists seeking a flavour of Olde England; and they are not disappointed. The half-timbered houses, pubs and shops near the bard's birthplace in the centre of Stratford have probably been photographed a million times. The cluster of Royal Shakespeare Theatres on the banks of the Avon draw in thousands of fans of his thirty-eight fabulous plays. Stratford is definitely worth a stop-over in May when the riverside gardens are in bloom, and outside dining is possible on a warm day. But our route along the Fosse drives past Stratford and joins the A429 all the way through the Cotswolds to the outskirts of Chippenham.

Felix and the Forest

To the right is the Heart of England Forest, though if you expect to see a massive wall of woodland you may be disappointed. The Forest covers a mosaic of habitats across 7,000 acres of Warwickshire and Worcestershire, with five main sites and 58 walking routes through the woods. It was the vision of a remarkable man called Felix Dennis, who died of throat cancer in 2014 at the age of 67. He left a thriving legacy. Felix was brought up in poor circumstances. His mother's house had "no indoor lavatory or bathroom ... no electricity, only gas and candles." He left home in his teens and earned rent by playing in rock bands and working as a sign painter. He began selling copies of the counterculture magazine, 'OZ', soon became a co-editor, and then became involved in the longest conspiracy trial in English history. He and his two co-editors had invited fifth and sixth- formers to edit a 'Schoolkids OZ' edition. They included a sexually explicit version of the Rupert Bear cartoon strip, (or should that be Rupert Bare?).

In 1971 this was too much for the authorities. The magazine offices were raided by the Obscene Publications Squad and the three editors were arrested and charged with 'conspiracy to corrupt public morals'. John Lennon recorded a single, 'God Save Oz/Do the Oz', to raise money for a defence fund.

At the end of the trial of 'The OZ Three', who were defended by the celebrated writer and barrister John Mortimer, the jury found them not guilty of 'Conspiracy to deprave and corrupt the morals of the young of the realm', but they were convicted of two lesser offences and sentenced to imprisonment. The convictions were overturned on appeal, and Dennis went on to found his own magazine company. It seems he instinctively understood the interests of the young baby-boomer generation, particularly of young men who were not catered-for by the conventional publishing world. As well as continuing with irreverent satire and humour, (Viz), he launched magazines about martial arts, (Kung-Fu Monthly), cars, (Carbuyer), computers, (Personal Computer World), and men's lifestyle, (Maxim, a title that began on the back of a beer mat and became massive in the USA), and many more. He also pioneered digital marketing and online magazines. While doing all that, he started writing poetry that became hugely popular, leading to poetry-reading tours across the UK and the USA, and then TV documentaries and best-selling books on how to get rich.

He used his money to sponsor university prizes, and helped the government of St. Vincent and the Grenadines to give every secondary school pupil a laptop. In 1995, Felix Dennis had planted a small wood near his home at Dorsington, just to the south of Stratford, and had the idea of establishing a large native broadleaf forest. The Heart of England Forest Ltd, a registered charity, now employs 80 staff and more than a million saplings have been planted so far. The aim is to buy up land and quadruple the acreage covered by the forest. Felix had bequeathed most of his fortune to the charity to make sure the project would continue and flourish long after his death. He is still present in his forest legacy in the form of a life-sized coloured statue standing near his grave.

Woodland Trust

Across the UK, the biggest charity planting native trees is The Woodland Trust. It was established, as it happens, at the same time as the OZ trial in the early 1970s, when environmental concerns were starting to take hold. Since then the trust's staff and volunteers have planted millions of trees across Britain, and have pledged to plant a million more in the next five years, 'each one with the potential to fight climate change, purify the air, prevent flooding, and of course be a haven for nature'. Native woodland is certainly a haven for some species that can't thrive without it. At the end of 2023, Defra, (The Department for Environment, Food and Rural Affairs), issued a report on the alarming loss of birds across the country, and it said woodland birds are in the steepest decline. The causes were said to be removal of hedgerows and the cutting down of areas of old woodland by landowners. Another cause is browsing by deer that remove the valuable understorey of scrub, bushes and new growth, leaving bare ground or nettles under the canopy.

The result is an overall decline in woodland birds of 37% in the past fifty years, and by 15% in just the past five years, which suggests the reduction of birds is accelerating. The species that rely on old deciduous woods in damp areas, are the worst affected. Numbers of the sparrow-sized lesser spotted woodpecker have dropped by 90% in the past 50 years. And these days you're unlikely to see the beautiful willow tit with its black cap and bib. They've declined 94% in the same period and have become extinct in most parts of South-East England where there has been most urban development. Prof Richard Gregory, from the RSPB Centre for Conservation Science, says, "Willow tits prefer scrubby, often wet woodland with lots of variety, so a decline in active woodland management and a burgeoning deer population means we are losing the understorey they need; in addition our soils are drying out as the climate changes and woods are becoming more and more fragmented with development pressure."

The willow tit is clinging on in parts of the Heart of England Forest, and of course there are some woodland birds that are doing alright, especially those that don't tend to feed in the scrub below the canopy. The great spotted woodpecker is thriving, and can sometimes be seen raiding the nut feeders in suburban gardens. And the lively nuthatch that leads an upside-down life for reasons best known to itself is happy scuttling along large branches and down the tree trunks, prising grubs from the bark with its strong bill. I think it's a brilliant bird with attractive slate-blue plumage and a snazzy black eye-stripe, and it has a very loud whistle that makes it easy to find in the woods. Numbers have increased significantly in the past fifty years, partly because the nuthatch is able to protect its nest holes from great spotted woodpeckers and the expanding population of grey squirrels that can gnaw their way into the nests to eat eggs or young. Nuthatches cleverly apply a circle of mud to the entrance holes in trees or nest boxes, leaving just enough space for them to squeeze in. When the mud dries, it's a solid barrier.

Introducing … the Dormouse

In some of the woods around here, The Woodland Trust, Warwickshire Wildlife Trust, the People's Trust for Endangered

Species and the Warwickshire Mammal Group have been working together to reintroduce one of our rarest and most delightful mammals. The tiny hazel dormouse – it's body is about the length of your forefinger – has soft golden fur and large black eyes, and is almost fully 'arboreal', which means it lives almost entirely in the trees, often quite high in the canopy, feeding on berries, seeds, nuts and caterpillars. So dormice are extremely difficult to see, and outside the summer months they are famously sleepy, as characterised in Alice in Wonderland at the Mad Hatter's Tea Party. The name is thought to come from the French *dormir*, to sleep, and regional names include dory-mouse, dozing mouse, derry mouse and seven-sleeper. In Devon it acquired the curious name of 'chestlecrumb'. When the weather starts getting chilly and the leaves are starting to fall, the dormouse makes its way down to the ground, builds a round nest of grasses and leaves, curls itself into a ball, and goes into a deep sleep called 'torpor', which can last as long as seven months.

According to a study by the University of Exeter, the numbers of the much loved creature had fallen by 72% in just over two decades, and they are now thought to be extinct in 20 English counties. Ruth Moffatt has devoted herself to saving the dormouse for many years. She organised the first reintroduction programme in Bubbenhall Wood in 1998. Ten years later she established the Warwickshire Dormouse Conservation Group in an attempt to find if there were any of the little rodents in the centre of England, and to encourage them, with more introductions and the installation of nest boxes and 2,500 home-made nest tubes attached to branches. In most places the search for evidence of dormice drew a blank, though there were some pockets of old woodland where they were found in small numbers.

In 2017 and 2018, 79 dormice from a captive breeding programme in Kent were released in Warwickshire across two different woodlands. Of course there wouldn't be much point unless the habitat is managed to help them, and volunteers have been coppicing and planting native trees to create a sustainable environment for the dormice. The selected areas of woodland must be joined together physically at the canopy level, to allow the mice to forage over a wide area. So hedgerow corridors of hawthorn and hazel linking the woodland are particularly valuable. Dormice are happy to raise their young in nest boxes, so plenty of boxes with protective metal plates round the holes were erected. The annual monitoring of the nest boxes begins this month and will continue into October. So far it's clear the populations are growing and spreading. Ruth Moffatt is delighted. She says, "Warwickshire could become one of the most important counties for dormice in the Midlands." Across the rest of the country, a small army of volunteers has released more than a thousand hazel dormice into 25 woodlands in the last 30 years. In some places they have even suspended rope bridges between clumps of trees to give the dormice a safe route to the next canopy. It's thought to be one of the longest running small mammal recovery programmes in the world.

Mouseman

There's an opportunity to see mice of a very different kind just a little further along our route. At Halford where the Fosse Way joins the A429 all the way to Cirencester, we can bear right to the village of Ilmington, past an upmarket pub-restaurant called The Fuzzy Duck. (I can recommend the gorgeous scallops and pea dish on their lunchtime menu). Ilmington has golden stone cottages with roses in the front gardens, and St. Mary's Church in the same deep gold. Approaching the church along a narrow walled path off Back Road, (and yes, there is a Front Road), the yews, Scots pines and limes in the churchyard are alive with twittering of goldcrests and blue tits and the call of the nuthatch; jackdaws shout their name from the square bell tower, while swifts newly arrived from Africa scream overhead. Inside, a beautiful round stone arch frames the chancel, and the wide transept has oak pews carved in the arts and crafts style. What makes them notable is that the wood carver was Robert Thompson, known as the Mouseman, because his signature, often hidden away in nooks and corners, was a carefully carved mouse.

He hailed from North Yorkshire, just like my family, but unfortunately I don't think he is one of my ancestors. He was a brilliant carver and carpenter, always working in English oak, and providing pews, chairs, pulpits and screens for a growing number of churches around the country as his reputation went before him. The mouse motif happened rather by accident in 1919 when he was working on a church screen and said to one of his colleagues, he was 'as poor as a church-mouse'. He carved a little mouse at the bottom of the screen to emphasise the point and did so thereafter on all his work. At St. Mary's Church in Ilmington there are 11 mice to find. It's fun to look for them; children love to go on a mouse hunt, crawling about between the pews. Now enormously admired, the Thompson style of oak furniture continues to be made by his descendants at a workshop and showroom at Leyburn in Wensleydale. I hope the Thompson family members are not as poor as church-mice. After all, these days a refectory-style oak table and 6 chairs from the Thompson workshops could cost you £24,000.

Further down the Fosse Way, south of Shipston-on-Stour - for hundreds of years a 'staging post' for stagecoaches running between Oxford and Stratford upon Avon - at Stretton on Fosse we slip into Gloucestershire. The ancient route drives straight down the wide High Street of Moreton-in-Marsh, proudly known as 'The Gateway to the Cotswolds'.

June

Moreton-in-Marsh to Cirencester

Think of England as a very large book.
The Cotswolds would be an unfussy chapter in the middle
somewhere where there is lots of limestone and even more sheep.
(Susan Meissner, American author)

Raven

The Cotswolds

This large area of rolling hills was designated as an AONB (Area of Outstanding Natural Beauty) in 1966, and at nearly 800 square miles is the third largest protected area in England after the Lake District and Yorkshire Dales national parks. The area certainly lives up to its AONB designation with outstandingly beautiful towns and villages made from the famous honey-coloured stone. Cotswold stone is a yellow oolitic Jurassic limestone, rich in fossils, particularly of sea urchins. The name 'Cotswold' is believed locally to mean 'the sheep enclosure in rolling hillsides', but students of Old English aren't so sure. The name could be derived from the 12th century *codesuualt* meaning Cod's high land. Cod was an established forename in Anglo-Saxon times.

Moreton-in-Marsh is in a low area next to the River Evenlode, a tributary of the Thames, with the rounded hills of the wolds all around; hence the marsh in the name. It has a very long history. Moreton is first mentioned in old documents as a Saxon settlement in the year 577, but before that, Roman coins and pottery found on the site indicate it was occupied during the construction of the Fosse Way. In medieval times it became affluent from the fleeces of the sheep grazing the nearby upland fields, and it was awarded a royal charter in 1227 allowing it to hold a weekly market in the wide High Street. To this day on Tuesdays, the market is packed with stalls selling local food, clothes, leather goods, jewellery, pots, pans and pottery, and is the biggest market in the Cotswolds. I find Moreton particularly attractive because it is full of independent shops, restaurants and cafes, with very few big retail chains in evidence. It also has some former coaching inns offering high quality food as well as the foaming beer.

The town has benefitted hugely from having a direct rail connection with London. It takes less than 90 minutes to come to Moreton from Paddington. So Londoners can enjoy a delightful day in the Cotswolds and be home in time for 'The One Show' or 'Coronation Street'. But in recent years, it has become a retirement destination for Londoners seeking a slower lifestyle, and more people working in the hurly-burly of London have decided they can move permanently to the Cotswolds and commute to London, especially with more working from home these days. Agents say buyers tend to be in their 60s, or people in their 30s, moving from London or Oxford, who are seeking a better environment for their young families. Property prices have gone up recently, so it is a bit hard for local families to buy a home, but there are a number of new developments on the edge of town with more affordable properties. A honey-coloured thatched cottage on the High Street is always going to be a bit steep.

The direct line to London isn't the first rail link from Moreton. Between 1821 and 1826, the Stratford to Moreton Tramway was constructed to link up with the canal network for the transport of Moreton's valuable cloth, and to bring visitors to the Cotswolds. The trams were horse-drawn for 35 years until steam locomotives were introduced and it was converted to a branch line railway. But by 1960, the branch line was deemed uneconomic, and on 2nd May 1960, the last passenger train chuffed into Moreton station. It had just one paying passenger. Since then the train service has been revived, the tracks have been repaired, station platforms lengthened, and at time of writing the Cotswold Line runs regular services to Hereford, Worcester and London.

Dazzling Raptors

Just outside Moreton there are signs to the Cotswold Falconry Centre. I've been to a number of bird of prey centres over the years, but this one is particularly impressive with 150 birds raised in captivity and looking in good condition. There are 60 different birds of prey looked after in the large aviaries, many breeding successfully. Some species are critically endangered in the wild. They include caracaras from South America, vultures from Asia and Africa, owls from Europe and the Americas, and of course some of our native birds of prey. Visitors can have the chance to put on a gauntlet and fly a large hawk. I can tell you it is pretty thrilling to see it take off from its perch and fly directly at you before smacking into the glove to take a piece of chicken. This is usually a harris hawk, a native of South America, rather like a small buzzard but with russet wings. The harris hawk is extremely cooperative, seeming to enjoy the company of people, so it's a favourite at falconry displays.

More jittery is my favourite, the peregrine falcon, with its powerful pointed wings and huge eyes. Watching a peregrine flying free then coming in for the falconer's lure is an unforgettable experience. The handler was a young woman who clearly had a very good rapport with the bird in her hand. When she had removed the bird's hood - it was a male or 'tercel', so-called because it is about a third smaller than the female falcon - he looked around keenly at the group of admirers, roused himself, (which means shaking his feathers to get them in order for flight), and off he went low across the fields, then climbing fast over the tress, scattering the wood pigeons, and out of sight. "This may take a while", said the falconer.

We all scanned the sky – which had patches of blue and pale clouds moving in a light breeze. After about ten minutes, she said, "There he is." "Where? Where?" The onlookers couldn't find him. Then through my binoculars I spotted this tiny dot against a cloud, like a little anchor printed on the sky.

The falconer began to talk to him – clearly for our benefit. "No, no, don't come in that way!" She explained that he shouldn't 'stoop' at speed with the wind behind him because there was a danger of him losing control and over-shooting the target. The bird was very aware of that of course, and travelled downwind, before turning, still not much more than a dot in the blue. The falconer started swinging her lure, "Come on then. Come on." He folded his wings and began to drop like a stone, then levelled out and hurtled low over our heads at well over 100 mph, with a sound like tearing cloth. Wow. She made him do two more circuits before throwing up the lure so that he could pick it off with those big yellow feet and land on the grass, 'mantling', which is when a bird of prey crouches over its kill with wings spread. The speed and power of the peregrine is awesome.

Batsford Arboretum

The Cotswold Falconry centre adjoins the Batsford Estate, with its famous arboretum and gardens. It was created in the 19th century by Algernon Bertram Freeman-Mitford, who had worked for the Foreign Office in China and Japan and had become an admirer of oriental landscapes. On his return to Britain he became Secretary to the Ministry of Works, which included Kew Gardens, increasing his enthusiasm for exotic plants and trees. When he inherited the Batsford Estate, it was his chance to create something special, and he wasted no time. He had the Georgian mansion knocked down and replaced by a neo-Tudor house that stands there today, and the mansion's formal gardens were ploughed up. He planted nearly two thousand trees and shrubs laid out in a 'natural' landscape. He had tons of rock brought in to make a ravine, with a watercourse running down the western side of the gardens and various oriental features nestling among the trees. There's a Japanese Rest House complete with a dragon on the roof to ward off evil spirits, a hermit's cave, and several bronze statues including two Japanese deer and a large Buddha imported by Mitford in 1900. By now he had become a Buddhist. In the summer, there are wildflower meadows in full bloom, and as autumn approaches, the arboretum will provide a brilliant display of flaming reds, salmon pink and rich purple foliage.

The estate and arboretum were inherited by Algernon's son, David Freeman-Mitford, and after changing hands several times, in 1985 the gardens were donated to a charitable trust that looks after them to this day, welcoming thousands of visitors and running a thriving garden centre. As for David who had inherited the gardens from their creator, you could say he had an interesting life.

Family Life with the Mitfords

Parents will always worry about their children, and hope they will do well and be happy. But David and his wife Sydney Bowles probably had more cause to worry than most. They had six daughters and a son. In the 1930s, the Mitford sisters in particular became notorious – rich aristocrats, well educated, talented, glamorous, unconventional and opinionated. Nancy divorced her husband when divorce was regarded as shameful, and went to France to live with the politician Gaston Palewski. She wrote many novels including 'The Pursuit of Love', and 'Love in a Cold Climate', based on her time at Batsford. Pamela married a millionaire physicist, but she too divorced to live with an Italian horsewoman. Diana married the aristocrat Bryan Guinness, but left him for the British fascist leader, Sir Oswald Mosely with whom she had two sons. The couple spent much of WWII in Holloway Prison. The fourth sister,

Unity, was an ardent admirer of Adolf Hitler, and when Britain declared war on Germany she was so distraught she shot herself in the head; but she botched the suicide attempt. It left her brain-damaged and the family packed her off to an island in Scotland where she died three years after the war had ended.

Sister number five was Jessica, who unlike the rest of her family was a dedicated communist. She eloped with Esmond Romilly and went to Spain to join the Civil War, eventually settling in the US where she became a best-selling writer. Her younger sister, Deborah, was also a prolific writer, but she was a little more conventional, marrying the immensely rich Andrew Cavendish, later to become Duke of Devonshire. With him she turned Chatsworth House into one of Britain's most successful stately homes. As for the only son, Tom Mitford, at Eton he had an affair with the writer James Henry Lees-Milne, then with a married Austrian dancer called Tilly Losch. He was also a supporter of fascism and refused to fight against Germany, so he was posted to the Burma campaign and died in action there. Batsford House is now privately owned and not open to the public.

Ancient Stones

After a wet spring, June is turning out to be dry and hot. Very hot. In the previous year the UK had recorded temperatures above 40 degrees celsius for the first time. The signs are that this year could be even warmer. The ground is now powder dry. There are news reports of silver carpets of dead fish in rivers and canals across central England. The reason is the low oxygen level in the water. Warmer water holds less oxygen. But also the relentless rain earlier in the year has produced run-off from fields and roads bringing various pollutants, such as waste from chicken farms that stimulates algae that consume oxygen.

So it is pleasant to take a short diversion from the Fosse Way to a breezy hill near Long Compton on the Oxfordshire border where mysterious rituals took place an amazing 4,000 years before the Roman era, in the Neolithic period, or New Stone Age. This was before the development of metal tools and artefacts, and when the nomadic hunter-gatherers began to settle as farmers. On this small grassy hill stand the Rollright Stones, a circle of limestone rocks, 30 yards across, which have been weathered over thousands of years into grotesque shapes. Throughout recorded history, the stones have been the subject of countless legends, folklore tales and mysterious events.

In fact there are three different monuments made at different times during the Neolithic and Early Bronze Ages. The first to be erected was a dolmen, a burial site for someone of importance, now called the Whispering Knights with the pillars that once supported a capstone leaning towards each other. Centuries later the stone circle called the King's Men was added to the site, and in the Bronze Age, the tall King Stone was erected. It's thought to be a grave marker. This hill above Long Compton has been a sacred site for hundreds of generations of our ancestors. The story of the Rollright Stones, as written in medieval times, was that an ambitious tribal king was marching his army across the Cotswolds intent on ruling the whole of England. He was confronted by a 'witch', said to be Mother Shipton in some tales, who said,

> "Seven long strides shalt thou take, and if Long Compton thou canst see, King of England thou shalt be."

But as the king gleefully strode forward, the ground rose up before him obscuring his view of the village below, and the witch cackled and said,

"As Long Compton thou canst not see, King of England thou shalt not be. Rise up stick and stand still stone. For King of England thou shalt be none; thou and thy men hoar stones shall be, and I myself an eldern (elder) tree."

And so it was that they were all turned to stone and she turned herself into a tree which is said to still grow in the nearby hedge. If it is removed, the King and his knights will spring back to life. The king became the King Stone, his men the King's Men stone circle, and his treacherous and conniving knights the Whispering Knights.

Another local tale recorded by the archeologist Sir Arthur Evans in 1895 is that some of the stones, notably the King Stone and the Whispering Knights, have been known to come down the hill at midnight to drink from the stream at Little Rollright Spinney. And fairies live under the stones apparently. But you only see them if you if have 'led a pure life'. So *that's* why I've never seen them! Here's another story. If you walk round the King's men stone circle and count the stones, you will never come up with the same number. I reckon it is 77. Or was that 75? The stones with their weird shapes have been used as a spooky location in quite a few films, and in 1978, a TV classic Dr. Who episode called *The Stones of Blood* had Tom Baker's intrepid time-traveller at the Rollright Stones confronting menacing walking rocks.

Summer Solstice

The stones may not really move, but they get plenty of respect at this time of year, at the Summer Solstice. Scores of people arrive in the darkness to watch the sun rise over the stones, and take part in rituals organised by the Cotswold Order of Druids, with the ceremonies led by the local Archdruid. Visitors are asked to join hands outside the King's Men circle and two druids create a gateway into the ring of stones with two long staves crossed at the top. The participants are allowed beneath the staves into the stone circle, and must walk round it three times before linking hands in the centre, and giving thanks for the sunrise.

As the sun rises, dancers dressed as fairies appear, while two druids offer the visitors sips of mead from goblets, murmuring, "Blessed be", and children offer plates of dried fruit, in a pagan form of communion. And finally a polished and carved stick of wood is produced and handed round. This is the 'Talking Stick'. It is said that when it is in your hand you feel the need to unburden your thoughts. Well at least you are expected to say where you're from, though some will recite a short poem extolling the power of nature, or say an extemporary prayer in praise of the sun that sustains all life on Earth. Certainly nature's spring renewal is clear to see at this time of year. The upland fields and roadside verges round here are sprinkled with vivid scarlet poppies, and the hedgerows are festooned with the red, white, pink and yellow flowers of the honeysuckle, the county flower of Warwickshire. Along the ditches and on damper ground in this arid summer, the tall purple loosestrife and cream candy-floss meadowsweet add to the tapestry of different colours, and the sweet scents of a still midsummer's day.

Return of the Raven

The calm weather means the sounds of birdsong carries further, with a skylark reeling above, and the deep croak-croak of ravens in the distance. There they go, a pair with their slow wingbeats carrying them straight across the valley of the Windrush. I think the old expression, 'as the crow flies', meaning in a straight line, must have referred to ravens rather than crows. The smaller and commoner carrion crows tend to wander somewhat in their flappy flight, while the raven seems to be more purposeful. Indeed, Norse legend speaks of Odin, the chief of the gods, having a pair of ravens who brought him important news from afar. Dressed all in black, and feeding on carrion, the raven is associated with ill-omen and death in classical and nordic folklore. It's said that flocks of ravens and crows had learned to follow a marching army, knowing there might be a gruesome feast to come. The collective noun for ravens is 'an unkindness'.

But this large bird was also thought to possess powers of prophesy, perhaps because like other intelligent members of the corvid family, ravens can be taught to speak, mimicking the human voice quite accurately. In stories, ravens often act as 'psychopomps', connecting the material world with the world of spirits. In Welsh mythology, the giant and god, Bran the Blessed, (that's not Brian Blessed by the way), had the raven as his totem and alter-ego, helping him to speak words of wisdom about the future. For reasons I haven't quite grasped, he issued orders for his head to be cut off, after which he could still speak words of prophesy. Legend has it that Bran's head was buried on the hill where the Tower of London was built. The ravens at the Tower are an echo of this ancient legend. I think it is wonderful to hear the deep croak of the ravens carried on the breeze, a sound heard only in the Welsh and Scottish mountains when I was a child, now heard across the whole of England as the raven numbers have increased along with the buzzards, mainly because gamekeepers no longer put out poisoned carrion.

Where the Wind Blows Cold

A short hop along the Fosse Way up an incline takes us to one of the main market towns in the area with an ancient history. The highest town in the Cotswolds, Stow-on-the-Wold, sits on the top of an 800-foot hill where no fewer than eight roads converge. It's a rather breezy location on the site of an iron age fort, and inspired the 18th-century couplet, 'Stow on the Wold, where the wind blows cold', which is etched on the walls of St Edward's Hall in the town centre. The elegant market square has an ancient cross at one end and the remains of the town stocks at the other. This important crossroads has been a trading post for a very long time, and since 1107 successive monarchs have granted Stow charters to hold fairs and markets, with woollen cloth traded in the market square, and huge numbers of sheep bought and sold. The 18th century novelist and travel writer Daniel Defoe reported that 20,000 animals were sold there in one day. The livestock would be herded into the square through alleys known as 'tures'.

The market town has flourished over the years, and as the wool trade declined Stow became the place to buy and sell horses. To this day the horse fair, sometimes called the Gypsy Horse Fair, attracts livestock dealers and traveller families from far and wide, some in the traditional caravans, and large crowds come to watch the parades and the auctions. The fairs are now held twice a year in a large field to the east of the town. Some locals say that the fairs attract a small anti-social element, mainly young men who drink too much, and many of the pubs and shops close during the fairs. But other residents of Stow and the surrounding area seem to welcome this traditional gathering with its colour, music and craft-stalls, not to mention some fine horses and ponies. The full version of the 18th century rhyme is:

> *Stow-on-the-Wold, where the wind blows cold*
> *Where horses young and old are sold,*
> *Where farmers come to spend their gold,*
> *Where men are fools and women are bold,*
> *And many a wicked tale is told,*
> *High on the freezing Cotswold.*

Four miles further down the A429 we pass the extremely picturesque villages of Upper and Lower Slaughter. The River Eye runs through the middle of both 'The Slaughters', with stone bridges connecting the communities on either side and a beautiful old mill at the lower village. The unusual name comes from the Anglo-Saxon, *slohtre*, meaning wet land. There are attractive fords at both villages, but the one at Upper Slaughter is deeper than it looks, so if there has been heavy rain and the river is running fast, it's advisable to take the circular road and cross the river on a bridge. The village hall in Upper Slaughter has a plaque with the names of the twenty-four young men and one woman from the village who left for the Western Front in World War I. Very unusually, they all returned safely, making Upper Slaughter one of a handful of 'Thankful' villages that lost no one in the Great War. In fact the village lost none of the thirty-six men who went to serve in World War II, making it a 'Doubly Thankful Village'. And it was a lucky place again in February 1944 when a Luftwaffe bomber unloaded 2,000 incendiary bombs on the village, but no one was killed or injured.

Bourton-on-the-Water

The Fosse Way crosses the River Eye at Slaughter Bridge, and the next stop is the ridiculously attractive Bourton-on-the-Water, with the River Windrush chuckling its way through the centre of the village and crossed by five little stone bridges. Locals like to call it, 'The Venice of the Cotswolds', and certainly there were Italians here once upon a time. Roman pottery and coins have been found in the village, where the Fosse Way connects with another Roman road, Icknield Street, running north into Yorkshire. There's loads to do on an outing to Bourton, with plenty to keep the children entertained. When they were small, my boys loved walking like giants through the model village, a detailed replica of the centre of Bourton in the 1930s, to a scale of 1/9th. There's even a model village in the model village. On the south side of the real village, another popular attraction is the Dragonfly Maze. This is a labyrinth of tall yew hedges but with an intriguing twist. There are fourteen clues on metal plates let into the pathways. These will guide you to the centre and a golden dragonfly hidden in an ornate pavilion. Once inside there is a final puzzle to be solved. The dragonfly and the puzzle within the maze were provided by the artist and writer, Kit Williams, who sprang to fame in the 1970s.

His book, 'Masquerade', contained lots of devilishly difficult clues that could lead the reader to a golden, bejewelled hare that he had buried in a casket 'somewhere in Britain' in a ceremony witnessed by the quizmaster of University Challenge, Bamber Gascoigne, who was sworn to secrecy. The nation was gripped. Where was the hare? The book sold over a million copies around the world. At one stage, Kit Williams was receiving 200 letters a day begging for more clues. It took three years before a pair of physicists worked out the answer and unearthed the golden hare in a park at Ampthill in Bedfordshire. Apparently the dragonfly to be found in the Bourton maze was made by Kit Williams from left-over gold and semi-precious stones after he had created the famous hare.

Parrots and Penguins

Next to the maze is the entrance to Birdland Park and Gardens, a fascinating wildlife park covering nine acres along the banks of the Windrush. There's an amazing variety of colourful birds in Birdland, including macaws, pelicans, flamingos, cassowaries, and the only British population of king penguins. (Some of them performed in the Hollywood film, 'Batman Returns', but only in non-speaking waddle-on parts). The large aviaries include a 'Desert House' greenhouse that has dry conditions favoured by some rare and threatened species. The park was created in 1957 by a keen bird-lover called Len Hill, known as 'The Penguin Millionaire'.

In 1970 he decided to buy two uninhabited islands in the Falklands archipelago, the Jason Islands, to provide some penguins for his growing collection. The owner was using the islands to graze sheep and offered to sell the lot for £10,000. Len told him he could keep the sheep, and bought the islands for £5,500. To help recoup some of the cost he issued Jason Islands postage stamps and even his own banknotes, featuring his portrait and signature, and pictures of various kinds of penguin, from the little jackass penguin (one pound note) to the King Penguin (twenty pounds). After his death, his family sold Birdland and the Jason Islands, but they remain as refuges for threatened species, with Livingston Leisure managing Birdland, and the islands bought by the American billionaires, Michael and Judy Steinhardt, who donated them to the Wildlife Conservation Society.

Rare Meadowland

The area surrounding Bourton is wonderful for walkers with a network of footpaths criss-crossing the countryside. There's a circular walk to The Slaughters, and nearby Salmonsbury Meadows is part of the 160-acre Greystones Farm nature reserve between the Rivers Eye and Dickler on their way to joining the Windrush. On a series of paths you can enjoy natural meadows and wildflowers and explore some of the history of this farming area. The meadows are a Site of Special Scientific Interest, (SSSI). The citation calls it one of the richest and largest traditional meadow systems remaining in the Cotswolds. The eleven meadows are divided by ancient hedges and some hedgerow trees, and support a range of rare plants, including southern marsh orchid, early marsh orchid, great burnet, cuckoo flower, pepper saxifrage and meadow rue. The reserve is owned by the Gloucestershire Wildlife Trust, whose volunteers manage the land with traditional haymaking and grazing by cattle. It's a great spot to visit at this time of year, with butterflies aplenty feeding on the flower meadows.

The A429 continues on its straight line south-west, crossing the A40 Oxford to Cheltenham road and the River Colne at Fossebridge, and through the market town of Northleach, with its imposing 'wool church' of St. Peter and St. Paul, dating from medieval times and considered the 'Cathedral of the Cotswolds.' One of the best kept secrets in the Cotswolds, Northleach is tucked quietly away from the busy A40. At the town's centre is the Market Place with some wonderful half-timbered buildings, relatively unchanged for 500 years. To the left of our route is Bibury, 'The most beautiful village in England' according to William Morris. I can't argue with that. The honey-coloured houses fronted with hollyhocks and roses are gorgeous. And the row of preserved 17th century weavers' cottages called Arlington Row has been photographed countless times, mainly by Japanese tourists who flock to the place where Emperor Hirohito chose to stay during his European tour in 1921. To the right is the village of Chedworth.

A Rich Man's Villa and a Rich Man's Cottage

In 1884, the foundations of a large Roman building were discovered at Chedworth. Excavations revealed elaborate mosaic floors, a large dining room, a heated west wing, and two bathing suites, one for damp heat and one for dry heat. It was almost certainly the home of a very wealthy Romano-Briton, perhaps a senior military figure. Chedworth was within horseback commuting distance from the great Roman centre of Cirencester just eight miles down the Fosse Way. Today the site is in the care of The National Trust with a visitor centre and information boards; it's regarded as one of the largest and most elaborate Roman villas in Britain.

Chedworth is also known for a very different building that made the news in the 1920s. Henry Ford, the founder of the Ford Motor Company and at the time the world's richest man after his mass-produced Model-T had sold in millions, became besotted with the Cotswolds during a visit to England. In Michigan he had established the Henry Ford Museum and nearby Greenfield Village, to preserve objects that were being lost in a changing society. He decided he wanted a Cotswolds cottage. His agent in Britain, Herbert Morton, recommended Rose Cottage in Chedworth, so-called because after rain the stone turned to pink. Henry said that would do nicely, and Morton bought the cottage for £500. But how to transport it to Michigan? If you are the richest man on the planet, nothing is impossible. The cottage was dismantled stone-by-Cotswold-stone. The keystones were numbered and packed into 506 sacks. The doors, windows, staircases and beams were packed into 211 crates, and it took a special train with 67 wagons to transport the 475 tons of material from Foss Cross Station to Brentford Dock. The pieces were shipped to new Jersey, then another train journey took them to the Greenfield Village in Michigan.

According to The Times, the villagers back in Chedworth 'viewed the whole proceeding with disfavour, not unmixed with indignation.' But for two of them it turned out to be a lucrative opportunity. The labour needed to rebuild the cottage was to be provided by Ford's factory workers, but he needed skilled craftsmen from Gloucestershire to supervise the work. Stonemason Tom Troughton and carpenter William Ratcliffe were sent to the USA on first class tickets, and stayed for six months in 1930 while Rose Cottage rose again. When the building was finished, Ford was delighted, and sent Troughton and Ratcliffe on a fortnight's holiday to Niagara Falls. He also paid them generously. With the money made from the trip, William Ratcliffe bought a piece of land in Bourton-on-the-Water and built two wooden houses for himself and his brother. The Chedworth cottage became a popular feature of the Henry Ford collection. He even imported some Cotswold sheep to graze decoratively nearby. It is said that the billionaire also wanted to buy the 15th century church of St. Peter in nearby Winchcombe, and the weavers' cottages at Arlington Row in Bibury, but strong local opposition and refusal to sell prevented him.

It's open country on either side of the A429 Fosse Way with honeysuckle climbing over the hedgerows and the meadow sweet in the verges seeming to wilt in the heat of this very dry June. In the fields there are lapwings dotted about, and some loose flocks on the move, flashing their black and white wings in the sun. They are good to see. A handsome bird with glossy green plumage and a long crest, the lapwing is one of the farmland birds that has declined seriously in recent years, and is now red listed. The British Trust for Ornithology reports that lapwing numbers in the UK have declined 60% since

1967. Intensive farming with two crops per year of cereals or grass hasn't helped this elegant plover, and increased numbers of buzzards and ravens have made nesting more perilous. But climate change must be a factor, with hot summers making the ground hard and dry. At the end of the month, the Met Office reports that this June has been the hottest ever recorded in the UK, beating the previous record by almost a full degree centigrade.

Ten miles further along our route we reach the market town of Cirencester, known as the Capital of the Cotswolds, and a significant centre in Roman times.

July

Cirencester to Chippenham

Dwell on the beauty of life... Think constantly on the
changes of the elements into each other,
for such thoughts wash away the dust of earthly life.
(Marcus Aurelius)

Emperor Dragonfly

Roman Cirencester

Cirencester, called *Corinium Dobunnorum* by the Romans, was the second largest town in Britain after *Londinium* during the 400 years of their occupation of England. The Corinium Museum in Park Street has the story of the development of the Roman town at this junction of the Fosse Way with two more ancient roads paved by the Romans, Akeman Street linking with Watling Street to the east, and Ermin Street that connected to the north with the legionary base at Caerleon in South Wales. There is a large grassed-over amphitheatre to the south-west of Cirencester, showing what an important Roman centre this was, bigger than Bath, Colchester and St. Albans. When the legions were withdrawn in the fifth century, the Saxons took over Cirencester and it became part of the kingdom of Mercia. In the year 628 AD, two Saxon kingdoms fought a battle for control of this strategic fortified town. According to the Anglo-Saxon Chronicle, the Mercian King Penda, (ruling the Midlands), fought armies led by the West Saxon kings Cynegils and Cwichelm in the 'Battle of Cirencester', but this fascinating chronicle of British history written in Old English by monks doesn't tell us who came out on top, just that there was 'an agreement'.

In the Middle Ages after the Norman invasion, wool made the town affluent. The church of St. John the Baptist, one of the largest parish churches in the country, was funded by the wool trade as were many of the churches in the area. Standing at the corner of a large market square, it is famous for its fan-vaulted ceilings, medieval glass, and wall paintings. The nearby Abbey was dismantled by Henry VIII's men in the 16th century. A bit of it remains in a park near the town centre. Cirencester is a lovely market town with a wide pedestrianised main street and independent shops selling local produce. The name 'Ciren' is thought to come from the

River Churn that flows through the east side of the town on its way to join the infant Thames a few miles away. How the name of Cirencester should be pronounced has varied over the years with 'Sistra' in past usage; today some local people simply shorten it to 'Ciren'.

South-west of Cirencester, the Fosse Way is interrupted by the Cotswold Airport, formerly RAF Kemble, and now used for pilot training and small commercial air traffic. To the west of the A429, the original ancient Fosse Way route goes cross-country straight as an arrow on narrow lanes until it rejoins the modern road system near Wraxall north of Bath. It is the border between Gloucestershire and Wiltshire. You can walk this section of the Fosse Way if you are feeling energetic. It's fairly flat all the way with views of the Cotswolds, and to the south the Somerset countryside and the distant Mendips. At Long Newton near Tetbury it passes over a lovely 18th century packhorse bridge. The 'Fosse Bridge' has the typical low parapets allowing horses and mules with bulky panniers to cross without their loads hitting the sides of the bridge. Then the track crosses the B4040 and passes over the young Bristol Avon. The number of Avons in Britain can be confusing. There are five in England, including the Warwickshire Avon, (as in Stratford-upon-Avon), three in Scotland and one in Wales. The reason is that in Celtic tongues, *avon*, or *afon* in Welsh, means river. So it is a pleonasm, a kind of tautology with repeated meaning: 'River River'.

Pests or Protein?

It's still hot in July but becoming more humid, with the threat of thunderstorms. Underfoot along this traffic-free section of the old Roman road, grasshoppers flick away and chatter to each other in the fields of wheat and barley. Grasshoppers and their close relatives the crickets are widely regarded across the world as pests. They are herbivores, favouring various grasses that include wheat, barley and other cereal crops. In warmer climes, especially in Africa, large locusts can appear in huge swarms that devastate farms in just a day or two and seem to be unstoppable. Here in England the arable farmers are a bit more relaxed about our little grasshoppers that produce the soundtrack of summer on a calm July day in the countryside. Their songs are known as stridulations. They are made by the rapid rubbing of legs or wing-casings against the wings. Surprisingly there are more than 25 species of grasshoppers and crickets in Britain. The species all have slightly different sounds, as with birdsong.

I've started to take an interest in grasshoppers, trying to name the different species. There are a few that we can all identify. The common green grasshopper is pretty obvious because it is common and it is green. Its sound is sustained, like the ticking of a bicycle wheel, for as long as 20 seconds. The meadow grasshopper can also be found anywhere there is long grass, and is also green on the upper body but it has brown wings and a dark tail. It emits a series of scratchy rattles. The field grasshopper prefers short dry grass and is also pretty common everywhere. It's brownish with a striped body. The crickets are less obvious, being quieter and preferring hedgerows, and in the autumn you might find one or two in your home as they seek a warm place to hibernate. The 'house cricket' can be a problem in that it likes to chew on material such as your clothes or soft furnishings, but most crickets, identifiable by their long legs, are harmless.

For centuries we humans have realised that grasshoppers can be an important source of food. In The Bible, Leviticus lists the foods that are approved and those that are to be avoided. For example:

> 'These are the birds you are to detest and not eat because they are detestable: the eagle, the vulture, the black vulture, the red kite, any kind of black kite, any kind of raven, the horned owl, the screech owl, the gull, any kind of hawk, the little owl, the cormorant, the great owl, the white owl, the desert owl, the osprey, the stork, any kind of heron, the hoopoe and the bat.'

As for insects, Leviticus disapproves of them as food, with the exception of grasshoppers:

> 'All flying insects that walk on all fours are to be detestable to you. There are, however, some winged creatures that walk on all fours that you may eat: those that have jointed legs for hopping on the ground. Of these you may eat any kind of locust, katydid, cricket or grasshopper.'

Perhaps the author knew that grasshoppers are exceptionally nutritious. They are about 40 percent protein, 43 percent fat and 13 percent dietary fibre. Fried grasshopper is eaten widely in Asia and Africa. In Mexico and Central America they are seasoned with salt, garlic and chilli, and used as toppings for pizzas and tacos. I've eaten dried grasshoppers in Japan, and found them crunchy and a bit chewy, but they didn't taste of much. Maybe they needed a dash of chilli. It's recorded that the Ohlone tribe of Native Americans living in California would light scrub fires to drive the grasshoppers into specially dug pits where they would be scooped up to cook and eat. It's recommended that the back legs which have some sharp spiky bits should be removed before eating, and apparently if you suffer from a seafood allergy they are best avoided.

Now, with the world population past eight billion and growing fast, there is a campaign to use more insects as foodstuff. In 2013 a United Nations report recommended that eating insects would help combat world hunger, and help to reduce greenhouse gases. Since then hundreds of commercial companies have begun operating grasshopper farms. They are relatively cheap to run, take up far less land than conventional farming, and have lower emissions than livestock or poultry. The report says insects are also 'extremely efficient' in converting vegetable feed into edible meat. 'Crickets, for example, need 12 times less feed than cattle to produce the same amount of protein.' It recommends farm-reared grasshoppers rather than wild ones, which may have ingested pesticides, or even heavy metals from the soil. I reckon we should dismiss any revulsion at the idea of eating some insects or the protein extracted from them. Two billion people eat them already, and they are regarded as delicacies in many countries. After all, not so long ago, lobster was regarded as food for the poor; now it is a pricey prized dish. The Romans are known to have eaten locusts and grasshoppers. And Beatrix Potter's Mr. Jeremy Fisher, after his failed fishing expedition, cooked dinner for his friends. *'Instead of a nice dish of minnows – they had roasted grasshopper with lady-bird sauce, which frogs consider a beautiful treat.'*

Gorgeous Gardens

To the right we can see the tall spire of St. Mary's Church in Tetbury, another impressive wool town. They still celebrate the fleece that brought wealth to the area with 'Woolsack Day' held on the last Bank Holiday in May with races through the streets and a fair. It is an area of Outstanding Natural Beauty, which is nice for King Charles III and Queen Camilla whose private residence Highgrove is nearby, with views across the southern Cotswolds to the Bristol Channel. In fact it's owned by the Duchy of Cornwall and control of Highgrove House was transferred to William when he became Duke of Cornwall as well as Prince of Wales after his father acceded to the throne. The gardens were famously redesigned by Charles himself and are cultivated with strictly organic methods. The grounds are open all through the summer and attract 30,000 visitors each year. But the house is firmly out of bounds.

Backing on to the Highgrove Estate are some other beautiful gardens that attract thousands of visitors. This is the National Arboretum at Westonbirt, established nearly two hundred years ago by the wealthy landowner Robert Stayner Holford, and now managed by Forestry England, a part of the Forestry Commission. It's a huge area of woodland and shrubberies criss-crossed by a network of pathways with all the trees labelled. There are an astonishing 2,500 different species and on a sunny day in autumn the display of red and gold leaves is a sight to behold. In the Silk Wood area of the arboretum, junior school children have been helping to plant hundreds of saplings, to replace those lost in a rather horrible cull of trees in 2021. Ash dieback had arrived.

Ash Dieback

The symptoms of the fungus appear at this time of year, with browning of the ash leaves, particularly in the crowns of the trees, and it will progress into the trunk producing dark lesions and preventing nutrients feeding the branches. So thousands of ash trees at Westonbirt had to be felled. Incidentally most of the timber from infected trees can still be used for furniture, flooring, joinery or sports goods such as cricket bats.

Ash dieback, also known as Chalara, came into Europe from Asia about 30 years ago, and the Northern European ash has no natural defences against it. The Woodland Trust estimates that 85% of our ash trees will be killed. The rest seem to have some kind of immunity. So after the felling of the ash trees at Westonbirt, the arboretum embarked on a major programme to replace them with 9,000 trees, and saw it as an opportunity to involve children from eight local schools. The project manager, Oscar Adams said, "Having the schools here allows us to excite young people about trees, woodland management and heritage conservation." I applaud wholeheartedly. Surely getting young children out of the classroom and involved in countryside management has multiple benefits, and should lead to a new generation of environmentally aware adults who value our biodiversity.

Malmesbury

The next town along the modern route of the Fosse Way is Malmesbury, lying in a strategic position on a hill in a protective loop between the Bristol Avon and the Tetbury Avon. Before the Romans arrived, there was an iron age fort on the site. This key position has made it a frontier town at different times with armed conflicts at its walls – Romans against Britons, Mercians against West Saxons, Anglo-Saxons against Danes, the 12th century Civil War, and later Royalists against Parliamentarians. In medieval times Malmesbury flourished as a market town, and in the broad square there stands a limestone market cross built in 1490. It is an elaborately carved octagon with open arches and stone benches to perch on. It's nicknamed 'the birdcage' by local people.

Today the notable feature of Malmsbury is its impressive Abbey, founded in AD 675 and rebuilt several times since. Aethelstan, The 'First King of All England', was buried there in AD 939. In the 12th century the abbey had an enormous spire – more than 400 feet high making it taller than Salisbury cathedral. The spire collapsed in the 16th century. Around this time the abbey managed to escape the worst of the destruction of religious houses during Henry VIII's dissolution of the monasteries, with the townspeople arguing that it was their parish church. The abbey is a magnificent building that still serves as the parish church of Malmesbury.

According to the 12th century historian 'William of Malmesbury', the abbey was the site of an early attempt at human flight. In the year 1010, a monk called Eilmer constructed a primitive hang glider, and holding on to it, launched himself from one of the abbey towers. Amazingly he didn't plummet, but flew 200 yards before crash-landing. He survived but broke both his legs. He doesn't get any credit in the history of human flight, because it seems gliding doesn't count. It took another 900 years before the Wright brothers managed the first powered flight. I can't help wondering why Eilmer did it. Perhaps he was testing his faith. If so, he certainly passed the test.

The Tiger Who Came for a Drink and Pigs on the Run

Malmsbury has had its fair share of curious stories. In 1703, a 33-year-old barmaid called Hannah Twynnoy didn't have a good day at work. She served customers at the White Lion Inn in the centre of town, and is believed to be the first person in Britain to be killed by a tiger. A travelling show or 'menagerie' had parked in the pub yard; the tiger would have been a very exotic and unusual beast in those days, the star of the show. How it got at Hannah isn't recorded, but her gravestone in the abbey churchyard seems to hint that she was cornered in the bar:

> *In bloom of Life She's snatch'd from hence,*
> *She had not room To make defence;*
> *For Tyger fierce Took Life away.*
> *And here she lies In a bed of Clay,*
> *Until the Resurrection Day.*

Escaped animals of a different kind made Malmesbury known around the world in 1998. A pair of Tamworth pigs from the same litter – brother and sister – were being unloaded at the slaughterhouse in Malmsebury when they made a bid for freedom, squeezing through a fence and swimming across the Avon. They hid in dense undergrowth and escaped capture for over a week. I've never worked for a tabloid newspaper, but as a journalist I know how tempting it is to seize on a story that brings a smile to faces, contrasting with the depressing and worrying main news of the day. And the tabloids and nearly everyone else went for the pigs-on-the-run story. NBC America flew in a reporter, as did NHK Japan. The 'Tamworth Two' were named Butch and Sundance after the famous outlaws.

They were captured after Sundance was spotted rootling in the garden of Harold and Mary Clarke. After being tranquillized with a dart, he (she) was kept overnight at a local vets. They told the press the staff had put chains and padlocks on the door to prevent any further escapes. Butch was rounded up by a posse the next day. The owner of the pigs, a road-sweeper, told journalists he still intended to send the Tamworth Two to slaughter. But enter the Daily Mail to save the day. They bought the pigs for an undisclosed sum in exchange for exclusive rights to their story, and installed them in an animal sanctuary. Did they know that interviewing the pigs may not have produced much useable copy? Never mind, the Mail had saved the bacon of the world famous Malmesbury porkers. Butch lived to the ripe age of thirteen while Sundance died a year later.

Time Stands Still

The A429 shadowing the old Fosse Way takes us through Corston, where there is an attractive little nature reserve around an old limestone quarry that filled up with clear groundwater and at this time of year is alive with dragonflies and damselflies. They are easy to distinguish as the smaller and slimmer damselflies fold back their wings when they settle. I find identifying the different species of dragonfly pretty difficult as they zoom past, but if they settle you can see the subtle differences on the thorax and abdomen of the types you are most likely to see here, the migrant hawker and southern hawker. The brown hawker is easy to spot – yes, it's mainly brown with golden wings. And here at Corston's Nature Reserve they have our largest dragonfly, the emperor, which has a green thorax and bright blue down the sides of the abdomen.

At the next village, Stanton St. Quinton, an ancient settlement with the remains of a Roman villa in its park, the old road goes under the M4, the motorway constructed between 1961 and 1971 to connect London with South Wales, and the Fosse becomes the A350 to Chippenham. But it is worth taking a short detour to the right to have a look at a village called Castle Combe, only because it is said by some to be the prettiest village in England. It is incredibly picturesque with honey-coloured cottages, old mills, a 14th century market cross with two village pumps, and the River Bybrook running through the lower part of the village. Walking into Castle Combe is like stepping back in time.

The parish council determinedly protects the village's traditional appearance. There are 107 listed buildings, and astonishingly no new houses have been built there since Shakespeare's time. So it's hardly surprising that Castle Combe is a favourite location for film and TV producers. It's been the setting for the film musical 'Dr. Doolittle', Agatha Christie's 'The Murder of Roger Ackroyd', the films 'Stardust' and 'The Wolfman', Stephen Spielberg's production of 'Warhorse', and many more – including, unsurprisingly, episodes of 'Downton Abbey'. The peace and quiet tends to be disrupted several times a year when events are held at the nearby Castle Combe Motor Racing Circuit, opened in 1950 on the site of a wartime airfield. All the great names from motor racing have wowed the crowds here, from Stirling Moss and Mike Hawthorn in the 1950s to Nigel Mansell and Ayrton Senna in the '70s and '80s.

Tiddleywink

Heading towards Chippenham, at a leisurely pace I'm sure, you could pop in to the tiny village of Tiddleywink. A few years ago it was in danger of being wiped from the map. For some reason the authoritative Bartholomew Gazetteer of Places in Britain ignored the hamlet, and its successor the comprehensive Collins British Atlas and Gazetteer also omitted to mention Tiddleywink. The last straw for the residents of the eight cottages in the village was that the local council didn't bother to replace the road sign at the entrance to Tiddleywink after it was damaged in an accident. So they launched a campaign to prevent the hamlet being swallowed up by the next village, Yatton Keynell. Heaven forbid! In 2003 the campaign was successful, the road signs were replaced, and you'll find Tiddleywink on your road atlas once more.

The origin of the name, goes back to the children's game, usually spelled tiddlywinks, which became rhyming slang for 'drinks', and according to the Oxford English Dictionary, evolved into slang for a small beershop. "I'm just stopping for a quick tiddlywink"- or - "I'm just dropping in to the tiddlywink." So the little village almost certainly got its name because one of the cottages served beer to the passing agricultural workers and drovers. From the hamlet of Tiddleywink it's just a three-mile hop across the Fosse Way into the substantial market town of Chippenham.

August

Chippenham to Bath

Sometimes I wonder what I'm gonna do
'Cause there ain't no cure for the summertime blues.
(Eddie Cochran)

Swallows

Chippenham and Alfred

Chippenham was well established even before the Romans arrived. It straddles an important crossing point of the River Avon, (that's the Bristol Avon), and the town has figured in many significant episodes of English history. In AD 878, the West Saxon King Alfred was staying at Chippenham with his family when the Danes, who were based in Gloucester, launched a surprise attack and Alfred had to flee into the Somerset Marshes. The legend of Alfred and the Cakes dates from this period. According to the story, he was given shelter by a woman who didn't recognise him. She told him to sit by the fire and watch some cakes for her, but he was so absorbed with his thoughts on how to defeat the Danes that the cakes were burnt and he was scolded. But the plan he was thinking about clearly worked. A few months later the Danish army was surrounded at the battle of Ethandun near the present day village of Edington and surrendered to Alfred at Chippenham.

Their King Guthrum was forced to accept peace terms which included him being baptised and taking on the Christian name of Aethelstan, with Alfred acting as Godfather. The Danes were dispatched to East Anglia where they were permitted to rule a Danish Christian kingdom under new laws known as The Danelaw. At Bratton near Edington between Chippenham and Warminster there is a monument in the form of a huge bolder, with a metal plate proclaiming:

> *To Commemorate the Battle of Ethandun*
> *Fought in this vicinity in May 878 AD*
> *When King Alfred the Great defeated the Viking army,*
> *Giving birth to English Nationhood.*

Chippenham was at the centre of the West Saxon's plan to unite the great kingdoms of Wessex and Mercia, partly through arranged marriages, in order to defeat the Vikings to the north. When Alfred was a young boy, his older sister Aethelswith had been married in Chippenham to King Burgred of Mercia, the midland kingdom. Later, after the Battle of Ethandun, Alfred's daughter Aethelflaed married the ailing Aethelred, Lord of the Mercians, who accepted allegiance to Alfred as King of the Saxons. When Aethelred died, the impressive Aethelflaed ruled in his place as 'The Lady of The Mercians', building a chain of forts to deter the Danes and creating educational establishments and rule of law.

From Fabric to Food

In medieval times Chippenham was a thriving market town. The A4 that runs east-west across the Fosse Way here was an important 14th century road that was essential for the English wool trade exporting cloth to London, and so its upkeep was funded in part by Bristol cloth merchants. But in the early 17th century, the town was badly afflicted by the plague, and with a downturn in the wool trade, the townsfolk fell on hard times. They turned to mixed farming rather than relying on sheep, and the area gained a reputation for quality meat and dairy products. In 1570, the Buttercross was erected on the square, with a roof supported by stone columns. It replaced the market cross where butter and cheese had been laid out for sale exposed to the elements. In 1889, the Buttercross was sold for £6 to the owner of the manor house in Castle Combe where it was used as a gazebo in his kitchen garden. A hundred years later, the Chippenham Civic Society managed to buy back the building for a little more than six quid – for £300 pounds to be precise – and after a long campaign it was reinstalled as the centrepiece of the town.

The arrival of the railway in the 19th century gave the place a big boost as fresh produce could be moved quickly to the big population centres, and the food giants Nestlé and Matteson's opened distribution centres in the centre of town. There are still markets in Chippenham every Friday and Saturday in the square, held in front of the 'Yelde Hall', a timber-framed building that has served as the town hall since medieval times.

Eddie and Gene

Chippenham made headlines around the world in 1960 when news broke that the American rock 'n roll star Eddie Cochran had been killed in an accident on Rowden Hill, part of the Fosse Way. He had become a global star with songs that captured teenage frustration, such as 'Summertime Blues', 'C'mon Everybody' and 'Somethin' Else'. A talented musician, he could play drums, guitar, bass and piano. He had just played the last gig of a UK tour at the Bristol Hippodrome with his friend and fellow rocker Gene Vincent, and was in a Ford Consul taxi on his way to London. Also in the car were Cochran's girlfriend, Sharon Sheeley, Vincent, their tour manager Patrick Tompkins, and the driver called George Martin who was just nineteen. An enquiry later concluded that Martin had been driving too fast, lost control, and smashed into a concrete lamp post. Cochran had thrown himself across his girlfriend just before impact, but was flung out of the car, (no seatbelts in those days), and he died later in hospital. The others all survived, though Gene Vincent had serious leg injuries.

A curious aspect to this story is that when the contents of the car were being held in the Chippenham police station, a police cadet called David Harman picked up Cochran's Gretch 6120 guitar, and spent some time playing it. Later Harman was to become known as Dave Dee, leader of the successful sixties band, Dave Dee, Dozy, Beaky, Mick and Titch. And I can't resist telling you another curious story. Four years later, the leather-clad Gene Vincent had recovered sufficiently to be able to return to the UK for an extensive tour which in July included the Wallington Public Hall in south London. I was the drummer in a local band called The Corsairs who were doing the warm-up performance. Gene Vincent's drummer didn't turn up. Apparently he was known for drinking vast quantities of whisky and passing out for hours. So at the very last minute I had to drum for the Vincent set, hoping I could remember his hits as he came on stage on crutches to huge cheers. So I can always say nonchalantly, "I played with Gene Vincent, you know."

Peacock Town

Here the Fosse Way takes its first major deviation from a straight line, branching to the right towards Bath on what is now the A4 through the attractive market town of Corsham. After the lucrative wool industry began to decline, Corsham became the centre of quarrying for 'Bath Stone', a hard limestone that was used to develop Bath in Regency style. During World War II, the extensive quarrying tunnels were used by the Ministry of Defence as bomb-proof operational centres, employing about 2,000 people.

Just off the High Street is Corsham Court, one of Wiltshire's finest stately homes with an impressive art collection and extensive gardens. The location was reputedly the site of a Saxon royal villa where, after Alfred's time, Ethelred the Unready ruled as 'King of the English' from 978 to 1013, a period of thirty-five years of conflict with the increasingly powerful Danes. Incidentally, the epithet 'Unready' is a mistranslation of the Anglo-Saxon, *unraed*, which means ill-advised.

The designers and renovators of Corsham Court are a lexicon of the top 18th century architects and horticulturalists – Robert Adam, John Nash, Robert Chippendale and the garden specialists Capability Brown and Humphrey Repton. Since 1779 it has been owned by the Methuen family, at time of writing by James Paul Archibald Methuen-Campbell, the 8th Baron Methuen. The house and gardens are open to visitors for most of the year. There are peacocks in the grounds, and they have a habit of flying into Corsham High Street and strutting about, disrupting the traffic, but also providing plenty of photo-opportunities as the peacocks fan and shimmer their tales, and the peahens wander about looking bemused.

Insects and Splatometers

Swallows with their long tail streamers are skimming across the lawns of Corsham Court while house martins chirrup and flutter above, both species hawking for flying insects. Unfortunately numbers of the beautiful swallows have been declining in recent years. According to surveys by the British Trust for Ornithology (BTO), swallow numbers in Britain were down 23 percent between 1995 and 2020, which was a particularly poor year, provoking letters to newspapers from farmers asking, 'where have my swallows gone?' The answer to the drop in numbers isn't entirely clear, but the BTO suggests one factor is the increase in stormy conditions during the swallow's 6,000 mile migration from South Africa, caused by climate disruption. Another very likely factor is the reduction in flying insects in recent years.

I remember that when I was a boy, after a trip in the car I would help my father clear the dead insects from the windscreen with washing up liquid and a cloth. These days there are very few splatted on the screen. And the drop in flying insect numbers isn't just anecdotal evidence. A recent experiment in Kent confirmed what we'd all observed. The charities Buglife and the Wildlife Trust asked members of the public to count the number of insects on their number plates, and they compared this to a similar study conducted twenty years earlier. The study organisers called the plates their 'splatometers'. Number plates are a standard size, so the data was pretty reliable. Results released in 2024 found that there were 78 percent fewer flying insects since 2004 – a dramatic reduction in just twenty years. Commenting on the survey, the Principle Curator in charge of insects at the British Museum said, "The results of this study are not surprising. Evidence of insect decline has been available for some time. Declines in woodland birds may well relate to the loss of insects in these habitats."

The experts believe one of the main causes of these declines is modern agriculture, with pesticides and chemical fertilisers killing insects, while the conversion of meadows, woodland and hedgerows into arable fields, some growing just a single type of crop, leaves less variety of plants for insects to feed on. Other factors such as air pollution and climate change are thought to be contributing to this worrying trend. Farmers must know they need pollinators. To my mind it's vital to retain some areas of uncultivated land and ideally to re-create insect-friendly habitats that are free of pesticides.

Flora and a Folly

There's evidence of Roman occupation all round the area approaching Bath. The A4 passes the large village of Box, where there are the foundations of a large Roman house.

There are more Roman remains near the next village of Bathford, where the ford in the name crosses the By Brook on the road to Batheaston, and nearby is a large meadow known as Horselands where it's said the Roman cavalry were exercised. Beside the Fosse Way but rather concealed by trees is the 'Three Shire Stones' monument that marks the boundaries between Wiltshire, Somerset and Gloucestershire - huge slabs of limestone with a capstone. The monument looks like a prehistoric megalith, but the stones were erected in Victorian times on the site of a Neolithic burial chamber. And to the left of the village on Bathford Hill I can see among the trees a tall rectangular tower dominating the skyline. It's Browne's Folly standing on the highest point in the area, with commanding views across Bath. The hill is a fine nature reserve managed by the Avon Wildlife Trust. The remains of Bath Stone quarries around the reserve provide varied and unusual habitats, with ferns on the damp cliff faces, pockets of ancient woodland, and rich flower meadows including nine species of orchid, among them the rare fly orchid.

In August these orchids are fading, but you might find one or two late flowering ones. Growing on a green spike, the blooms of the fly orchid certainly look like flies, with petals remarkably like wings and a head with antennae. But they are not trying to attract flies. The orchids emit a scent that mimics the pheromones of a female digger wasp. The male wasps try to mate with these deceptive flowers, dusting themselves with pollen in the process, and when frustrated, buzz off to try a new orchid which they duly pollinate.

The Day's Eye

On the short grass beside the paths, there are sprinkles of white, like confetti after a wedding. This is one of my favourite flowers. It appears in March and continues to flower for 8 months of the year. The humble daisy is pretty, medicinal and rich in ancient folklore based on love and fertility.

In Old English, the daisy was called the 'day's eye' because at night or in dull weather, the petals close over the yellow centre, and during the day they open. So the expression, 'fresh as a daisy', suggests you've had a good night's sleep. In Norse mythology, the daisy is Freya's sacred flower. Freya is the goddess of love, beauty and fertility, so these little flowers came to symbolise childhood, motherhood and new beginnings. For the Romans who quarried here, the daisies represented purity and innocence. In Roman mythology, Vertumnus, the god of gardens, became enamoured of a nymph called Belides. In order to escape from his advances she turned herself into a daisy, hence the scientific name, *Bellis perennis*, the second word meaning year after year of course. In 'Hamlet', Shakespeare used a daisy chain to represent Ophelia's innocence. Daisies can be eaten - their leaves are sometimes added to salads - and are traditionally used medicinally. Wild daisy tea is used to treat coughs and bronchitis, and it's said that daisies applied to a wound will help it to heal.

As for Browne's Folly itself, it was built in 1848 on the instructions of Wade Browne, a Yorkshireman who had taken on the lease and lordship of the manor of Farleigh Down. The land included the cluster of limestone quarries. There are various stories about why he constructed the tower. One is that it was an act of charity giving employment to quarry workers during a downturn in the business. I tend to believe the less altruistic version that it was a huge advertisement for his high-quality stone, called 'Bath Stone' because over many centuries quarries all along this belt of limestone have supplied the materials that have given Bath its distinctive appearance. It is a hard form of oolitic limestone, laid down during the Jurassic period about 150 million years ago when this part of Britain was covered by sea. Fragments of shells and sometimes small sea creatures are often found in the stone. An important feature of Bath Stone is that it is a 'freestone' that can be sawn in any direction to make building blocks, unlike other types of stone that have formed in layers, such as slate. For over two thousand years, it has been used to construct the fabulous buildings that have made Bath a World Heritage Site.

September

Bath to Shepton Mallet

"I really believe I shall always be talking
of Bath, when I am at home again I do like
it so very much....Oh! Who can ever be tired of Bath?"
(The naïve Catherine Morland in Jane Austen's
'Northanger Abbey'.)

Nuthatch

Aquae Sulis

The Romans who had conquered the cold and wet island of Britain must have been overjoyed to find natural hot springs near a river leading to the sea routes to mainland Europe. And there was a ready supply of high-quality building material already being quarried to pave the Fosse Way that crosses the River Avon here. The water bubbling up in the geothermal spring originates as rain on the Mendip Hills, which percolates through the limestone to a depth of two and a half miles. Geothermal energy heats it up nearly to boiling point, and under pressure the water rises through fissures and the Pennyquick geological fault to emerge at a comfortable 46 degrees celsius – over a million litres a day.

At the warm spring, the Britons had established a small shrine to Sulis, the goddess of healing. The Romans wasted no time in developing some elaborate baths to provide R&R for the officers supervising the construction of the Fosse Way and for the nobles building villas protected by its garrisoned forts along the ditch and road. Lead to line the baths was also readily available from the mines in the Mendips to the north-west of the Fosse. By AD 60 a substantial town had grown up. The Romans called the place, *Aquae Sulis*, which means the waters of the goddess Sulis Minerva, who would look after you like a mother, and they adopted her shrine at the spring. It seems she could use her powers to punish anyone who wronged you.

Archeologists have found 130 lead and stone tablets inscribed with curses addressed to Sulis and thrown into the spring. Some talk about clothes being stolen while their owner was having a bath. Many were written in code, with backwards writing or words in the wrong order. One, when decoded and translated from a local form of Latin says, 'Docimedis has lost two gloves and asks that the thieves responsible should lose their minds and eyes in the goddess' temple.' After the collapse of the Roman Empire, the Anglo-Saxons called the town *Akemanchester*, meaning the aching man's city, reflecting the reputation the springs had for healing the sick. But the locals tended to call it *Bathum* or *Bathan* meaning 'at the baths', and by the middle ages it had become simply 'Bath'.

Warm Bath

Six million people visit Bath every year, making it one of the top tourist destinations in England. If you haven't been one of those visitors, you've been missing a wonderful city, and it takes a stay of several days to do justice to this UNESCO World Heritage Site. There's an efficient park-and-ride scheme to avoid getting tangled up in traffic, and a popular open-topped bus tour where you can hop on and off anywhere along the route to explore all the main landmarks. Much of the architecture is from Bath's 18th century boom years as a fashionable warm-water spa, with fine houses built from the warm creamy stone, including the spectacular Royal Crescent, regarded as one of the greatest examples of Georgian architecture. Built between 1767 and 1775 by the influential architect, John Wood the Younger, it is 500 feet long, containing 30 Grade-1 listed houses and the sweeping curve is fronted by a lawn overlooking Royal Victoria Park, with a ha-ha that would have kept the grazing livestock away from the house without a fence or hedge disturbing the idyllic rural view.

Other attractions in this extremely attractive city include the Pulteney Bridge over the Avon, designed by Robert Adam to connect the estate of the Pulteney family with the city, and built with shops along both sides. It's one of only four bridges of this kind in the world, with the Rialto in Venice being perhaps the most famous. The river is picturesque, but if you fancy a cold bath in the river by the bridge, I wouldn't advise it. Analysis in 2024 showed that the Avon at Bath is one of the most polluted stretches of river in the country, with Wessex Water struggling to clean up its act. The restaurant in the nearby Pump Room serves sumptuous afternoon teas, and there are countless festivals and performances throughout the year celebrating Bath's vibrant arts scene. The magnificent Bath Abbey Church where in the year 973, Edgar was crowned King of All England, is certainly worth a visit.

Dashing Nash, Jane, and Buns

Among many notables buried in the nave of Bath Abbey was Beau Nash, the dandy and leader of fashion who became Master of Ceremonies at the assembly rooms, vetting those who hoped to attend the balls, acting as a matchmaker, and establishing the strict rules of dress and etiquette that were followed around the country for most of the 18th century. It would be an understatement to call Nash a colourful character. He was known to have a string of mistresses, and despite counselling young men not to engage in risky games of chance, was a compulsive gambler himself. Heavily in debt from gambling, he was forced to move in with his mistress Juliana Popjoy. When he moved out, Ms Popjoy was so distraught that she spent the majority of her remaining days living in a hollow tree. Marking her death in 1777, a local newspaper reported:

> 'The celebrated Juliana Papjoy [sic] ... in her youth had been the mistress of the famous Nash of Bath, and after her separation from him, she took to a very uncommon way of life. Her principle residence she took up in a large hollow tree ... resolving never more to lie in a bed, and

*she was as good as her word, for she made that tree her
habitation for thirty or forty years.'*

The Assembly Rooms where Nash reigned as the self-styled
'King of Bath' are now owned by the National Trust who
organise tours and events there. Jane Austen danced there
frequently when she and her parents were living in Bath
between 1801 and 1806, and she featured the Bath society
balls in Persuasion and Northanger Abbey. But she never really
liked the place, and wrote to her sister, Cassandra, 'It will be
two years tomorrow since we left Bath for Clifton, with what
happy feelings of escape!' I think she would have been amazed
to know that after 200 years, there would be a Jane Austen
Centre offering 'Ten Jane-y Things to Do', and this month it is
the annual Jane Austen Festival, with plenty of dressing up and
Regency dancing.

A young Jane wrote in a letter from Bath that she had been
'disordering my stomach with Bath bunns', meaning she'd
been eating a few too many. The extra letter 'n' on the bun was
a deliberate reference to Sally Lunn's buns, that were eaten at
the popular breakfast parties, and you can still get them at
Sally Lunn's Eating House in North Parade Passage, in one of
the oldest houses in the city dating from 1482, and where in
the 17th century Sally created her famous buns. Her real name
was Solange Luyton. She was a Huguenot refugee escaping
persecution in France, and introduced her light, brioche-like
bun to Bath high society. Versions of the Sally Lunn Bun can
be found now around the world, from the United States and
Canada to Australia and New Zealand. But the original is
deemed to be by far the superior version, at least in Bath.

It's thought that the Great Exhibition of 1851 gave birth to
the 'London Bath Bun'. Records show that 943,691 'Bath
Buns' were consumed over the 6 month period of the

exhibition, but the Sally Lunn kitchen is scathing about the London version. 'They are small, doughy, stodgy and overpoweringly sugared. They also keep miserably.' Elizabeth David, who wrote the definitive book, 'English Bread and Yeast Cookery' in 1977, declared, "Sally Lunn buns with their delicate and light personality differ greatly from a version downgraded by bakers into the amorphous, artificially coloured, synthetically flavoured and over-sugared confections we know today." She was talking about the so-called London Bath Bun. So there you are. If you fancy a real Bath Bun, go to Bath.

Wartime Bath

The exiled Emperor Haile Selassie of Ethiopia, who traced his roots back to King Solomon and the Queen of Sheba, spent four years from 1936 to 1940 living at Fairfield House in Bath, after Mussolini's troops had invaded his country. His warnings about the intentions of the Nazi Axis powers generally went unheeded, until the outbreak of WW2. Shortly after Winston Churchill had replaced Neville Chamberlain as Prime Minister, Mussolini declared war on Britain. Churchill approached Haile Selassie to go back to Ethiopia to support British-backed troops and help to defeat Italian forces in north east Africa. In June 1940 the Emperor left the south coast on a secret flight to Egypt under the pseudonym of Mr Strong. Eventually he made his way to Sudan. After a frustrating wait of several months he was able to enter the Ethiopian capital, Addis Ababa, as a returning hero on 5th May 1941, five years to the day since Italian troops had first captured the city.

A year later, the war came directly to Bath with a series of three raids in quick succession by the Luftwaffe, known as 'The Bath Blitz'. When the sirens sounded, many people didn't take cover believing it was one of the regular air raids on Bristol. But this was the start of the 'Baedeker Blitz', aiming at places of historical or cultural significance rather than military installations, as a reprisal for the destruction of the city of Lübeck. On two nights in April 1942, 417 people were killed with 1,000 injured and 19,000 buildings were damaged, including part of the Royal Crescent and most of the city's churches. The Circus and Paragon Georgian Terraces were destroyed and the Assembly Rooms were burnt out. After the war it took many years for all the damaged building to be restored; there was a shortage of skilled workers and of the correct materials needed to ensure that the rebuilding of the centre of Bath was faithful to its elegant Georgian style.

Prior Park

The modern road following the Fosse Way out of Bath is the A367, taking us through rolling Somerset countryside with fruit orchards towards Radstock, Shepton Mallet and Yeovil. On leaving Bath there are signs on the left to the Prior Park Landscape Gardens owned by the National Trust. The Palladian mansion on a hill overlooking the gardens and beyond to the city skyline of Bath was built by a remarkable man called Ralph Allen. In the early 18th century, he started work as a post boy in his grandmother's post office in Cornwall and by the time he was just nineteen he had become a postmaster in Bath. A few years later he had taken over the franchise of the South-West postal business and introduced a range of reforms and efficiencies. For example before Allen's reforms, nearly all post went to London to be sorted before being delivered round the country. He took over more and more regional post office contracts, and it's estimated he saved the GPO a million-and-a-half pounds over 40 years.

He became immensely rich, and promptly made a second fortune by buying quarries and mines providing Bath Stone for the expanding spa city. In 1742 he was elected Mayor of Bath, and used some of his fortune to establish schools, the 'Mineral Water Hospital' in central Bath, and community centres, but he had enough left over to buy the nearby Claverton Manor, and to have a summer home built overlooking Weymouth harbour. I don't think the former post boy was shy about his success. He moved out of the city centre to the splendid mansion built at Prior Park with its rare Palladian Bridge spanning a lake in grounds landscaped by Capability Brown. He built it on a hill overlooking the city, "To see all Bath, and for all Bath to see."

Combe Down Tunnel

Lying underneath the south-eastern suburbs of the city is an old railway tunnel that carried an extension of the Somerset and Dorset Main Line from Bath Green Park Station under the hills to emerge at Combe Down Village. The tunnel is just over a mile long, making it the longest in the country with no ventilation shafts along its length. It is quite narrow because when it was built in 1874 it was unaffordable to make a tunnel wide enough for two lines. There was a gradient inside the tunnel, all of which made the single track line quite a challenge in the age of steam. The line was restricted to freight traffic - passengers would not have to endure the choking smoke in the tunnel – and the goods trains running south from Bath were often 'banked', meaning there was a second locomotive pushing at the rear. The banking loco would uncouple at the entrance to the tunnel and return down the gradient to Bath.

It was rare for trains to be permitted to travel in opposite directions on a single track line, so to ensure no problems, the driver of the first locomotive carried an 'electric tablet' and the banking engine had a 'staff', both of which had to be connected to the appropriate signalling equipment before any more trains could be allowed on that stretch of line. Nonetheless, on 20th November 1929, there was a fatal accident, but not because there were trains travelling in opposite directions. A northbound goods train had a particularly heavy load and was travelling slowly when it entered the tunnel. The driver and fireman became overcome by smoke and fumes and collapsed in the cab. When the train passed the summit of the gradient, it ran away at high speed and crashed into the goods yard at the station in Bath, killing the driver and two railway workers. The Inspecting Officer at the subsequent enquiry recommended a lower maximum load for freight trains, and that there should always be a banking engine to ensure decent speed through the tunnel.

In 1966 the line closed, along with hundreds of other branch lines around the country. After repair and restoration financed largely by the Sustrans walking and cycling charity, the tunnel is now part of a 'greenway' route, with LED lighting and a cycle-friendly surface, making it the longest cycling tunnel in Britain.

Fine Weather Fine Wine

The weather in September is unseasonably warm. In fact it is sweltering, peaking at more than 30 degrees celsius for a full week in England. With the south coast beaches crowded, the newspapers are full of stories about the heatwave and an 'Indian Summer'. Incidentally the expression 'Indian Summer' has nothing to do with colonial India; it is first recorded on the 18th century relating to Native Americans, though no one is quite sure what it indicated apart from a warm autumn.

The jet-stream has curled north bringing southerly winds from the Sahara. In fact they are bringing some of the desert with them. The occasional shower is full of orange sand, coating parked cars across southern England. At the end of the month, the Met Office will release figures showing that it was the warmest September in the UK on record. It ties-in with global average temperatures that have also been running at record levels. With sea temperatures around our coasts also measured at higher than ever levels, and the polar ice melting faster than previously recorded, there are a signs of global warming everywhere.

To the west of the Fosse Way beyond Bath you can stop at one of Britain's growing number of vineyards. They have sprung up across southern and central England as our summers get warmer, and winters are less severe. At the last count there were nearly 950 vineyards in Great Britain, many specialising in English sparkling wine that in recent years has won awards for its quality. The Lower Conygre Vineyard near Peasedown St. John on the Fosse is a relatively new addition to the English wineries. A little further west is the larger and well-established Corston Vineyard Estate which offers tours and tasting sessions. I should say that other vineyards are available.

So did the Romans plant vineyards in England during their 370 year occupation? They certainly quaffed large quantities of wine, according to historians and archeologists. But there is little evidence that they grew the grape on these shores, which would have been a struggle because of the harsh climate, and the Britons favoured beer and mead. The Romans preferred to import the fine wines from conquered Gaul, many shiploads coming in to Exmouth at the southern end of the Fosse Way. It was the Norman medieval period that saw vineyards appearing in the south of England and the Midlands, often in the grounds of monasteries where the monks needed wine for the altars. At least that was the excuse! The Domesday Book of 1086 records 42 vineyards in England, twelve of them attached to monasteries.

The wine-producers were certainly aided by the 'MWP'. Historians use these initials to refer to the Medieval Warm Period affecting North Atlantic regions from AD 900 to 1300, before very cold winters returned. Man-made climate change is now helping a boom in wine production in more northern parts of Europe. There are several successful vineyards in Norway, with the most northerly near the ski resort of Telemark. And even Finland has recently decided to develop viticulture.

The Somerset Coalfield

Our route down the Fosse Way, which would have seen wagonloads of wine conveyed from Exmouth and Exeter to the Roman troops garrisoned along its length, brings us into coal mining country, which is difficult to imagine when looking at the rural landscape with sheep dotted about on the foothills of the Mendips. There's some evidence that the Romans dug out coal around here in 'drifts', possibly for use in lime kilns making mortar. The ancient town of Radstock had been a small staging post on the Fosse Way, but it grew rapidly in the 18th century when coal was much in demand. By the 19th century about 4,000 people were employed in the Somerset Coalfield. Seventy-nine collieries were opened producing well over a million tons of coal per year. The coal was of good quality but came in narrow seams which were difficult and dangerous to work.

The Radstock Museum in the former Market Hall tells the story of the coalfield, with a candle-lit recreation of a mine showing how hazardous it was for men and boys, some as young as five, to work seams which could be as little as two-feet high. The museum has an impressive sculpture outside that is a replica of a pithead 'sheave wheel', to remind visitors of the region's mining heritage. The last two pits were closed in 1973 because of competition from more cost-effective mines and falling demand. Interestingly, the spoil heap of Writhlington Colliery on the east side of Radstock is now a Site of Special Scientific Interest, because it includes 3,000 tons of Upper Carboniferous rock from which more than 1,400 insect fossil specimens have been recovered.

Murders Galore

Just beyond Radstock is the picturesque town of Midsomer Norton, with the River Somer running through the centre. It is assumed to be the model for the series of crime novels by Caroline Graham. When in 1997 the screenwriter Anthony Horowitz adapted her 'Chief Inspector Barnaby' series for the hugely successful TV series, 'Midsomer Murders', he borrowed the name of the town, and used the names of surrounding villages to create the fictional County of Midsomer. It proved to be one of the most dangerous places in England.

Throughout the span of 136 episodes, there have been more than 415 murders, 603 deaths in total, and an additional 168 attempted murders or suicides. The formula of peaceful rural English life and picturesque villages that secretly seethe with violence was an instant hit. The first episode, 'The Killing at Badger's Drift', was watched by 13.5 million people, and the producers never looked back. 'Midsomer Murders' has been sold to more than 200 countries around the world. But strangely none of it was filmed in Midsomer Norton. The producers preferred the picturesque Chiltern villages closer to London.

A couple of miles to the south is Stratton-on-the-Fosse straddling the old Roman road. It was a thriving village during the coal mining years that brought significant income to the Radstock area. At Stratton you must visit the Downside Abbey Church. It's huge and hugely impressive, with a tower rising 180 feet and dominating the landscape. At first sight you might think it had medieval origins, but in fact it is one of the great neo-Gothic buildings of Britain, started with typical Victorian confidence in 1840, constructed in phases, and finally completed in 1935. It features the work of several distinguished architects. Thomas Garner, Sir Ninian Comper and Sir Giles Gilbert Scott all contributed to its beauty and originality.

Harridge Woods

Now some of the former mining areas have been taken over by the Somerset Wildlife Trust. For example, Harridge Woods near Nettlebridge on the Fosse Way, is a series of woodlands called Harridge Woods East and West, Home Wood, Edford Wood and the Keeper's Cottage, known for its bats. The reserve is a large area with traces of its mining history everywhere. There are overgrown spoil heaps and some shafts dating back to medieval times. In the early days miners excavated the valuable coal by using bell pits. These were vertical shafts dug down until they hit the coal seam, then a wide area round the foot of each shaft was cut giving it a bell shape. The miners must have used ladders to get down to the seam, and they winched up the waste in buckets called kibbles. Fifty-two bell pits have been found on the reserve. Now the Harridge Woods reserve comprises a series of woodland blocks along the valley of the River Mells, with volunteers helping to restore the original broadleaf woodland.

In the 1950s and '60s the old woods were mostly cleared and the area was planted with conifers and poplars, particularly in Harridge Wood East. But the timber business didn't thrive, and now with the Wildlife Trust thinning out the conifers to allow natural regeneration and clearing the overgrown riverbank, the wildlife is returning, with the green and great spotted woodpecker, nuthatch and goldcrest all seen or heard in the growing canopy of deciduous trees, and grey wagtail, dipper and kingfisher are now regulars along the Mells River. The dilapidated Keeper's Cottage was bought in 2006 with funding from the Heritage Lottery Fund, and it has been made secure, mainly for the benefit of the bats that roost there every year. It is home to seven species of bat – Greater Horseshoe, Lesser Horseshoe, Brown Long-Eared, Natterers, Daubenton, Pipistrelle, and the very rare Barbastelle. Unfortunately the reserve has been badly affected by ash dieback. At time of writing it is closed while felling of affected trees can take place.

A mile further south, the A367 Roman Road links up with the A37, which will follow the old route all the way to Ilchester. The first stop is the cider town of Shepton Mallet.

October

Shepton Mallet to Ilchester

*The heat of autumn
is different from the heat of summer.
One ripens apples, the other turns them to cider.*
(Jane Hirshfield, American poet)

Muntjac

Sheep Town to Cider Town

Approaching Shepton Mallet there are signs to the left for the historic house and gardens of Kilver Court. In many ways the last 400 years of the town's development is encapsulated in this single building. It was built in 1650 as a country house for the Whiting family who were making their fortune from the nearby woollen mills. When cheaper imports threatened the Somerset wool business, the mills at Kilver Court were converted to 'silk throwers' and then to the production of lace. During the 20th century the site became the centre of a successful brewing business, and later the headquarters of the leather-goods manufacturer, Mulberry. Now it is a shopping complex, or 'retail outlet', with the gardens overlooked by the spectacular Charlton Viaduct with 27 arches spanning the River Sheppey; this section of the Somerset and Devon Railway was closed in 1966. I've never quite understood how a manufacturing centre, making high quality things to be sold around the world, can switch to making its income from shopping. But I'm not an expert in macro-economics.

The name Shepton comes from the Old English *scoap* (sheep) and *tun* (farm, town or settlement). The Mallet part comes from the Norman Malet family who were granted the area not long after the 1066 Norman conquest. So perhaps we should pronounce it '*Sheeptown Mallay*'. Nowadays locals simply call it 'Shepton'. There is lots of evidence of Roman occupation here, halfway between Bath and Ilchester on the Fosse Way, including pottery kilns, brooches, hoards of coins from the 1st and 2nd centuries, and burial sites.

The Amulet

In 1990 there was excitement in archeological circles when an amulet, (normally worn around the neck to protect the wearer from evil), was unearthed from a Roman grave dating from around AD 400. The object was a disc with a Chi-Rho symbol representing Christ's name in Greek mounted on a silver cross. The amulet was regarded as a significant find. Shepton Mallet's theatre was even renamed 'The Amulet' in honour of the remarkable early Christian object.

In 2008 the metal of the amulet was scientifically analysed. The chemical analysis revealed that the silver had been refined in the 19th century or even later. Unfortunately the amulet is a hoax. Why it was made and placed in the grave remains a mystery. Those responsible have never come forward. Perhaps someone visiting the Glastonbury Festival four miles away enjoyed making silverware in the early Christian style, and thought it would be an amusing idea to put one in the archeological dig. But there's another theory.

The excavation of the Roman settlement at Shepton and its cemetery was in advance of a building development planned for the site. Some local people believed that the development work should cease, that the remains of the Roman town should be preserved and the site opened to the public on a permanent basis as a museum, with all of the tourism benefits that this would bring. A petition signed by 650 people was sent to Chris Patten, the then Environment Minister, and to the Archbishop of Canterbury, in an attempt to stop the building work. Perhaps the discovery in a Roman grave of a rare early Christian silver amulet would tip the balance of the argument? Who knows?

Wool and Silk

Shepton Mallet has flourished from the sheep in its name for many centuries. When Henry VII needed money to fund his military campaign against the Scots in 1496, he called on the affluent wool merchants of Shepton Mallet specifically, *'to make loan to us the som of ten pounds whereof ye shal be undoubtedly and assuredly repayd'*. I doubt if the wool merchants were repaid.

At the height of the cloth trade in the 17th and 18th centuries, there were said to be 50 mills powered by the River Sheppey in and around the town. When the local industry declined, mainly because of the steam powered mills in the north of England undercutting their prices, the town switched to the manufacture of silk and crepe. Shepton mills made the silk used in Queen Victoria's wedding dress. When wool, cloth and silk production declined, the Shepton industrialists had to adapt again. 'What have we got? Abundant clean water – barley – hops – fruit by the wagonload.' The answer was, of course, brewing.

Apples and Pears

The Anglo-Bavarian Brewery built in 1864, and still an imposing local landmark, was the first in England to brew lager. For a clientele used to brown beer or dark stout, this yellow stuff might have seemed a bit weak and – dare I say - foreign. But its refreshing qualities were liked, and at its height it was exporting nearly two million bottles around the world. Lager has become a staple tipple in every pub in the land. But when the brewery closed in 1921, out-competed by a host of other lager breweries in different countries, Shepton adapted again and turned to the Somerset fruit orchards.

To this day it is a centre for cider production, including Blackthorn that uses only local bitter-sweet apples. In 1992, the four Showerings brothers set up a factory at the former Anglo-Bavarian Brewery, and 'Brothers Cider' is now sold around the country and abroad. They were keeping the brewing tradition in the family. Their parents had established

Shepton as the home of Babycham, made from pears. There's a giant yellow chamois outside the factory. The cute Babycham fawn was designed in 1957 by John Emperor of the advertising agency CDP, part of the marketing plan aiming the sparkling drink at women, who in the postwar years were going into pubs and bars, previously the domain of men. Babycham became the first alcohol advertisement and the second ever advert to appear on British television, alongside Colgate toothpaste. The first was for another toothpaste - Gibbs SR. I suppose that reflects the fact that the state of the nation's teeth in the '50s was pretty poor.

The Babycham slogan, 'Genuine Champagne Perry', caused some disquiet among the French champagne producers and Bollinger sued the company. The legal action was unsuccessful, with the judge deciding there could be no confusion between champagne (12% alcohol) and champagne perry (6%) and through the 1970s and '80s the Shepton product went from strength to strength. At one stage the factory was turning out 144,000 bottles an hour. The profits helped to pay for the landscaping of the gardens at the company's headquarters at Kilver Court. Babycham has fallen out of fashion in recent years; perhaps women think it's a bit patronising. In February 2024, Brothers announced that they will be re-launching with 4 new flavours. They are App-Solutely Pear-fect, Un-Berrylievable, Best of the Zest and Berry Sub-Lime. They will be available only in cans. No more pretty bottles. Will these new flavoured drinks prove popular? We will see.

A Roof and a Grave

In 2016 a survey by National Express coaches voted Shepton Mallet the fifth 'most loved market town' in the UK. (It lost out to Ross-on-Wye, Thirsk, Grantham and Bedford. In sixth place was Chippenham, so the Fosse Way claimed two of the top six places). In the centre of Shepton is a tall market cross in the pedestrianised Town Street, overlooked by the imposing tower of the Church of St. Peter and St. Paul. Dating from the 12th century, the magnificent church speaks of the wool-trade years that made the town affluent. Its most striking feature is the arched 'wagon-roof' over the nave, with 360 oak panels and 36 angels carved in the early 16th century. The architectural historian, Nikolaus Pevsner, in his monumental 46-volume guide, 'The Buildings of England', regards the Shepton Mallet church as having the finest example of a wagon-roof in the country.

Just south of Shepton on the Fosse Way is the hamlet of Cannard's Grave. So who was Cannard with his grave commemorated? Was he a significant landowner or perhaps a holy man? On the contrary, local legend has it that in the 17th century he was the publican of a local inn and a thoroughly nasty piece of work. Known as 'Tom the Taverner', he had been robbing his guests, thieving from nearby properties, smuggling and forging documents. After his trial he was hanged from the gibbet at the crossroads next to the inn and buried nearby. A more likely story is that the grave is that of Kendred or Kennard, the last man in England to be hanged for sheep-stealing. Some of his poor countrymen may have considered execution a trifle harsh and wanted to remember him. A few years back, the Cannard's Grave Hotel changed its name to the Cannard's Well Hotel, because they had a well in the grounds, and because the former name was less than inviting. Especially as 'Kennard' was said to haunt the place.

Arrivals from the North and East

The A37 heading pencil-straight towards Ilchester passes through the curiously named village of Hornblotton Green, notable for its attractive Arts-and-Crafts Church of St. Peter, and where the Monarch Way crosses the Fosse Way. The monarch in question was Charles II, and the long distance path is supposed to follow his winding route from defeat at the battle of Worcester to his escape to France from Shoreham Harbour in Sussex, hiding in an oak tree along the way. After Lydford-on-Fosse, the Fosse Way joins the busy A303. The weather is still unseasonably mild after a record warm September. The temperature is up to 23 degrees celsius in early October, followed by a successions of cold fronts from the south west. A brief change to easterlies brings several million winter visitors.

The hedgerows are suddenly alive with chattering birds, feasting on the hawthorn berries. The thin whistles of the redwings and the 'chack-chack' of the fieldfares tell us that the winter thrushes have flown in from Scandinavia, Eastern Europe and Iceland, travelling long distances to avoid the harsh winters there. It's estimated that 700,000 redwings spend the winter in Britain and a similar number of the larger and more colourful fieldfares. Recently, a handful of these winter visitors have stayed to nest in England. Our warming climate may encourage more to breed here in coming years. The winter thrushes are numbers 72 and 73 on my bird list for the Fosse Way year. They are joined by loose flocks of starling and blackbirds that have crossed the North Sea, while from the woods the rasping calls of jays collecting and burying acorns indicate that autumn has truly arrived.

Roadkill

Unfortunately, along this stretch of road there are quite a few bodies. Dead badgers are at the side of the road every few miles it seems, along with foxes and the occasional deer. Most have been struck by vehicles at night. I have hit a badger in my car in the dark. It dropped down from the verge into my headlights and 'bang', instant death for the poor badger and a large insurance claim for me to repair the front of the car. What it must be like to hit a deer I can't imagine. September and October are the main months for the deaths of wild animals on our roads, apparently because young animals are exploring to find their own territories. In recent years, roads have had a major impact on our wildlife. The 'Road Lab', a team of researchers at Cardiff University, has been studying roadkill for some years. The researchers have been collating 'citizen science data' sent in by members of the public, to understand the relationship between roads and wildlife.

In 1951 there were 4.2 million vehicles on the UK's roads. In 2021 there were 39.2 million vehicles registered with the DVLA. So it's hardy surprising that collisions with motor vehicles are the biggest cause of mortality for badgers (50,000 per year), hedgehogs (up to 300,000 per year) and pheasants (an estimated 6 million annually). So far the Road Lab has received 90,000 roadkill records. It seems the autumn months are particularly dangerous for grey squirrels and muntjac deer. But the predators and scavengers have certainly benefitted from this perpetual slaughter. The large amount of roadkill is one of the main reasons for the increase in buzzards and ravens across the country, and the success of the red kite introduction project.

A fair number of humans also eat roadkill. Arthur Boyt from Cornwall was the subject of TV documentary which featured him casseroling badger and poaching a polecat. He died in 2023 at the age of 83 – not from food poisoning. He had cancer. The chef, Sean Rowe has a popular Facebook site where he shows how to make roasts and pies from animals or birds found on the road, and a blog with advice on what to pick up and what to leave alone. It's all pretty obvious really. If it looks diseased or has been partly eaten, leave it. And he says by far the most important thing is to cook it *thoroughly*. But is it legal to pick up roadkill? There seems to be some misunderstanding about that. Here's the relevant part of the Wildlife and Countryside Act.

> *S11 (2). If any person...*
> *(e) uses any mechanically propelled vehicle in immediate pursuit of any such wild animal for the purpose of driving, killing or taking that animal ... he shall be guilty of an offence.*

Sean Rowe says it seems to him that accidental collision does not apply. A dead animal in the road is the property of the landowner, in most cases this will be the local council, and there is almost no objection from councils to people removing dead creatures. The blog emphasises that you must not stop to pick up something if there is any danger to other road users or yourself. My brother-in-law occasionally picked up freshly killed pheasants. He served roast pheasant to his mother-in-law, and warned her to watch out for any lead shot. A little joke that he enjoyed.

Deer

The deer that seem most vulnerable to traffic are the gingery muntjacs. About the size of a Labrador, with striped faces and small horns, you can sometimes see them casually browsing on the grass verges apparently unconcerned that they are yards from thundering lorries. At night watch out for their eyes. Deer have a reflective membrane at the back of the eye. This membrane, called the *tapetum lucidum*, is what causes the eye-shine of deer caught in headlights. Muntjac numbers are increasing rapidly. They were introduced from China to Woburn Park in Bedfordshire in the 19th century, and escaped individuals started breeding in the wild little more than 100 years ago. Now they are spreading north in some numbers, and can be a major pest – destroying young trees and the understory in woodland that is so important for many species. They can eat all the flowers in your garden if you live near a ribbon of woodland, as I can testify.

There are six species of deer living wild in the UK. The Romans would have hunted just two of them – the native species: the red deer, the largest mammal in Britain and the beautiful roe deer with its pale coat and white bottom that flashes as it runs away. By the 18th century, the roe deer was almost extinct in England and Wales because of hunting. Now it is the commonest deer in Somerset. The fallow deer with its spotted back was almost certainly introduced by the Normans. The others are more recent introductions – the Sika brought into British estates from the Far East in 1860, and the Chinese water deer with a pale coat and tusks rather than antlers. They escaped from Whipsnade Zoo in Bedfordshire in 1929 and have now spread across the Midlands and South-West. So how many deer are there now in Britain?

The Mammal Society and DEFRA reckon there are at least 2 million and the numbers are growing, boosted by the pandemic period when the commercial market for venison collapsed and there was less culling. The environmental writer, George Monbiot, catalogues a number of other reasons. He cites, 'Less poaching, new woodlands and plantations, warmer winters, autumn sowing providing young crop plants for deer to eat all year round. But above all because there are no effective means of controlling them.' He argues that human efforts to control deer damaging crops and woodland, such as fencing, contraception, and shooting, are proving ineffective. He argues for the reintroduction of their natural predators, wolves and lynx. With the farmers vehemently opposed to such an idea, I can't see that happening, so regulated shooting or culling seems to be the only answer. Perhaps non-vegetarians should eat more venison. The British Deer Society says, 'Venison is a great source of protein, incredibly low in fat, and its levels of saturated fat are much lower than in other red meats like beef. It also contains minerals that are good for our health, including iron, phosphorus, potassium, and zinc as well as vitamins B6 and B12, riboflavin, niacin, and thiamine. It is one of the healthiest meats on the market.'

November

Ilchester to Honiton

To be ignorant of what occurred before you were born
is to remain always a child.
For what is the worth of human life, unless it is woven into
the life of our ancestors by the records of history?
(Marcus Tullius Cicero)

Sparrowhawk

Ilchester

Ilchester has a rich history. It was an important location in Roman times called *Lindinis*. In AD 60, the invaders constructed a timber-walled fort to guard the Fosse Way's crossing point over the River Yeo, and later encircled the town with stone walls. A lot of mosaic floors have been unearthed in the town, showing it was occupied by affluent Romans who decorated their villas. During the 12th century it was the county town of Somerset. Now Taunton holds that title, but Ilchester retains a ceremonial mace decorated with three kings and an angel, dating from the thirteenth century. It is the oldest staff of office in England. The mace can be seen at Ilchester Museum at the Town Hall House that is on the Fosse Way just behind the Town Hall.

During the English Civil War in 1645 the town was the scene of several clashes between Royalist and Parliamentary forces fighting for control of the bridges over the River Parrett and River Yeo before the Battle of Langport, eight miles to the west. Following its success against King Charles I at Naseby, the Parliamentarians' New Model Army under Sir Thomas Fairfax destroyed the last Royalist field army here. It was a key moment in the First Civil War; the Royalist forces were severely depleted, allowing the Parliamentarians to press on to take Bridgewater, and then to storm Bristol.

Which Way for the Fosse Way?

From Ilchester, the route of the Fosse Way is followed by the A303 towards Exeter, and passes below the earthen ramparts of the impressive Bronze Age and Iron Age hill fort of Ham Hill. It was captured in AD 45 by the Second Legion led by the future emperor, Vespasian, during his conquest of the

Durotriges tribe in Dorset. The site is now marked by a tall obelisk that is a memorial to the men from nearby Stoke-sub-Hamdon who died in the two world wars, and the whole hill fort site is a popular country park visited by a quarter of a million people each year. In the summer the wildflower meadows are full of butterflies, and the woodland walks are alive with the sound of birds claiming their territories. In the winter there are soaring buzzards and occasional flocks of golden plover dashing across the wide open skies.

At Petherton Bridge over the River Parrett, the original Fosse Way route follows country lanes to the south of the A303 and after Ilminster it becomes a little more difficult to follow precisely, partly because there are several Roman roads criss-crossing this area. There are two branches of modern roads from Ilminster into Honiton. The more direct route is along the A303 and A30. The more southerly ancient route takes us along the A358 through Chard and to the carpet town of Axminster.

Chard

Chard was written as *Cirden* before the Norman Invasion. It was a substantial Saxon settlement. I don't know how familiar you are with Anglo-Saxon spelling and pronunciation, but I went through it at university, and here's a bit of useless knowledge for you. The letter C as in Cirden would have been pronounced as a Ch. The hard C ('K') and the soft C ('Ch') depended on the vowel that followed it. So the old name of *Cirden* was pronounced *'Chirden'* or *'Chaerden'*. It is one of the highest towns in Somerset; in fact it is a watershed. There are streams on either side of Fore Street, one heading north towards the Bristol Channel and the other ending up in the English Channel to the south. After the Anglo-Saxon and

Roman eras, the town has had a chequered history, flourishing despite many setbacks. Most of the town was destroyed by fire in 1577, and it was further damaged during the English Civil War, notably in 1644 when Charles I and his troops spent a week in the town. Forty years later it was at the centre of a bold attempt to seize the throne of England.

In 1685, James Scott, the Duke of Monmouth, landed at Lyme Regis. He was the illegitimate son of Charles II, and as a Protestant was pretty miffed that the Catholic brother of Charles, James II, had taken over the throne. Monmouth had a lot of local support from the staunchly Protestant west country. In Chard he was proclaimed king before a cheering crowd. But his enterprise came to a sticky end with his troops bogged down at the battle of Sedgemoor and heavily defeated by the Royalist army. After the collapse of the rebellion, Chard witnessed the execution of 12 of the Duke of Monmouth's rebels, who were summarily tried and condemned by Judge Jeffreys. They were hung, drawn and quartered by the 'Handcross Tree' whose site was near the present Tesco roundabout. The tree was removed to make way for the railway in 1864 despite local protests.

Just before the outbreak of the Second World War, a bomb-proof bunker was built behind the Chard branch of Westminster Bank at number 7 Fore Street, to hold duplicates of important documents in case the headquarters in London was destroyed. It was also used to secretly store the emergency banknote supply of the Bank of England, though rumours that the Crown Jewels were also held in the vault have never been confirmed.

The town has a long history of manufacturing, notably of textiles, then in the 19th century, it was lace, when manufacturers from the Midlands decamped to escape from the Luddite riots when lace-making machines were smashed by angry workers trying to protect their jobs. These days one of the larger local employers is Numatic International Ltd. that makes the red 'Henry' vacuum cleaners with the slightly mischievous smiley face. Unlike most of its competitors, such as Hoover and Dyson, the firm continues to manufacture in Britain, with the factory operating continuously and churning out 4,000 products a day. Hooray for Henry.

Just a mile to the north side of town is the large Chard Reservoir, a local nature reserve run by Somerset Council. The 92 acres include mixed woodland, wildflower meadows, and reed beds, with a bird hide on stilts protruding into the water to give good views of the varied bird life on the water and on the fringes of the lake. In winter the usual ducks, geese, cormorants and grebes are in evidence, along with some less familiar species. The great white egret is regular here, along with the cattle egret, now moving north rapidly from its usual haunts in North Africa and mainland Europe. And on the muddy shoreline there are common and green sandpipers, and occasionally the rare spotted redshank. An elegant wader, slightly larger than the common redshank, it migrates from its breeding grounds in northern Europe and Siberia to spend the winter here. The Chard Reservoir with its woodland paths is a valuable piece of accessible green space, just a short walk from the town centre.

Pattering Gulls

We are heading for Axminster. It is pretty well established that this was on the original Fosse Way route. It is still very mild for the time of year. The trees are hanging on to their leaves and have turned golden. Then a cold blast from the north at the end of the month says goodbye to the 'Indian Summer' and temperatures drop to below freezing at night in the English Midlands.

Across the open fields, black-headed gulls are 'pattering' for worms. They dance on the spot for a while, then step back and wait for the worms to appear. It seems the worms are convinced it has started to rain, and they love to take in some moisture. People sometimes wonder why gulls are inland. "It must be stormy at sea." Well, many gulls spend their lives inland. Black-headed gulls nest in noisy colonies on islands in lakes and rivers, and generations of farmers have seen them following the plough in the autumn months.

Suddenly the gulls all rise in unison, calling, and the sky is a whirling mass of birds - small tight flocks of starlings, twittering groups of goldfinches, and wood pigeons clattering towards the nearest trees. There's a raptor about. Then from behind me, quite low, a large female sparrowhawk with its characteristic flap-flap-glide cruises past with a couple of crows close behind. It has been spotted, and swiftly moves away on powerful wings. But the birds all stay in the air. Magpies are chattering. Five minutes later they are still wary. I look up, and there she is – a dot or little cross high in the sky surveying the scene, looking for an unwary meal. Then she slides away on the breeze at amazing speed and is gone. The sparrowhawk, like many predators, must kill every day.

Coaches and Carpets

The original Fosse Way was a little to the east of the A358 to Axminster, with the route now followed by the B3167 passing in a straight line through the hamlets of Street and Perry Street where it is still called Roman Road, and joining the modern main road at the village of Tytherleigh. The name is first recorded in 1154 as *Tiderlege*, an old English word meaning a thin woodland. There's plenty of mixed woodland here along the valley of the River Axe as it makes it way to the sea at

Axmouth. The market town of Axminster is named after the impressive Norman church, now 'The Minster Church of St. Mary the Virgin' and the town's parish church. Arriving in Axminster, we cross from Somerset into Devon, with its rolling countryside and high hedges.

Axminster dates back to Celtic times and for the Roman invaders it became an important crossroads protected by a fort, with Roman roads leading away to Lincoln, Seaton, Exeter and Dorchester. In the 18th century, it was on the busy coaching route from London to Exeter. More than 16 coaches a day would stop at the George Hotel in the main street, so that passengers could refresh themselves, (and probably go to the loo, I imagine), while the coachmen changed the horses. Axminster was also on the so-called Trafalgar Way, the name given to the historic route used to carry dispatches with the news of the 1805 Battle of Trafalgar from Falmouth in Cornwall to the Admiralty in London. In these days of mobile phones, it's difficult to imagine the king and the government waiting for days or even weeks to know if they were about to be invaded. Nelson's hand-written bulletins would need a fast cutter to get from the fleet to Falmouth, then a succession of horsemen clattering their way non-stop to London. There is a plaque commemorating The Trafalgar Way in the town centre.

Whitty and Dutfield

But the main claim to world fame of the name 'Axminster' is its reputation for high quality carpets. The man responsible was a local weaver called Thomas Whitty. In 1755 he was visiting Cheapside Market in London when he spotted a large Turkish carpet and admired its colour and quality. Back in Devon he worked for months to develop looms that could produce similar complex patterns, and on Midsummer's Day completed his first carpet. The workers paraded it through the town and the bells were rung at the Whitty family's chapel. The beautifully patterned woollen carpets were immediately popular with the aristocracy and they were soon adorning the Royal Pavilion at Brighton, Chatsworth House, and various castles including Powderham and Warwick. The business received a significant boost when King George III and Queen Charlotte visited the factory and bought some rugs, and soon Axminster carpets were being exported around the world, the most famous being a huge carpet for the Topkapi Palace of the Sultan of the Ottoman Empire - modern day Turkey - surely a wonderful example of taking coals to Newcastle.

In 1828, disaster struck. A fire destroyed all the weaving looms and a few years later, the company owner, Samuel Whitty, the founder's grandson, was declared bankrupt. But nearly a hundred years later, a chance encounter on a train was to revive carpet-making in Axminster. A Scottish carpet manufacturer called Harry Dutfield, based in Kidderminster, was finding business a bit of a struggle during the thirties depression. He must have been doing ok because he was on his way to The Motor Show to buy a Jaguar. On the train he got chatting to a vicar from Devon who mentioned that Axminster no longer made carpets. Dutfield decided to move his operations to Axminster, and revive the famous name. In 1937 he persuaded British Railways to extend its station at Axminster and lease him some nearby land to build a factory. After the war, during which the factory had been making aircraft parts, carpet weaving got into full swing.

In 2005, Axminster Carpets Ltd marked 250 years of carpet-making in the town by producing a large commemorative rug. It was paraded through the town by the weavers in traditional fashion to much applause, and was blessed by the Bishop of Exeter. The carpet is now in Clarence House, the London residence of King Charles and Queen Camilla. You can learn all about the town's carpet-making history at the Axminster Heritage Centre in 'Thomas Whitty House' in Silver Street.

Honiton Lace

Leaving the town towards Exeter along a short section of the A35, our route links up with the A303, and the Fosse Way spears straight through the centre of the major market town of Honiton. Most of the buildings are Georgian, with elegant symmetrical lines, because in 1747 and again in 1765, the town was ravaged by fires that swept through the old timber-framed buildings. The High Street sloping down to the valley of the River Otter is dominated by the 104-foot-tall tower of the Parish Church of St. Paul. It was built in the 19th century on the site of a medieval church – the Allhallows Chapel - and has seating galleries all the way round, as was the style in early Victorian times, to accommodate more people when congregations were much larger than today. Next to the church stands the former chancel of the old chapel. It's one of the oldest buildings in Honiton, dating from 1326, and it is now a fascinating museum, run entirely by volunteers. The building itself is beautiful, with a curved roof decorated with painted panels. Beneath the decorative roof is an eclectic range of objects from Honiton's history dating back to Neolithic times, with well-preserved stone and antler tools, some 6,500 years old. There are some items even older than that - fossils from archeological digs in the area, the most famous being the Honiton Hippo. The fossilised remains of seventeen hippos were found during the construction of the bypass in 1965. The hippos are thought to have lived in the area during a warm period before the last Ice Age, when England had a climate similar to that in Africa today. Also on display are examples of the town's famed pottery, hand-painted with flowing forms from nature, and there's a finds table from the local metal-detecting club with military buttons, some from the Civil War days.

But a couple of steps down into a lower room you find the main display in the Honiton Museum, or to give the building its full title, 'The Allhallows Museum of Lace and Local Antiquities'. For it is lace that made the town's reputation. The hand-made lace on display is pretty breathtaking. The work required to make a shawl embroidered with flowers, leaves, birds or butterflies in fine detail took years. Honiton lace is called 'part lace', with the various motifs made separately, then attached to a net ground. But the net itself was made by hand and was incredibly intricate, until machine-made net came to the fore in the 19th century. The local industry received an enormous boost when Queen Victoria ordered a bridal dress trimmed with Honiton lace. On display in the museum are some dazzling examples of hand-made lace, including some black lace worn by the Victorians as a symbol of mourning and a rather racy scarlet nightdress which was owned by Wallis Simpson. King Edward abdicated the throne to be with her in 1936. My volunteer guide said she herself had learned how to make lace in the traditional way, and had embarked on a Christening shawl that she said should be ready in seven year's time.

Hot Pennies

In 1221, Honiton was granted a Royal Charter by King Henry III allowing it to hold a weekly market. To celebrate, the town held a fair, but it seems farmers and farm workers were reluctant to come to town in case the bailiffs arrested them for outstanding debts. So the Mayor declared that during the week of the fair, no arrests would be made for unpaid debts. It was a neat move; the Honiton Fair became hugely popular. The landowners and gentry took to throwing hot chestnuts from upper windows to the children below, and over time this changed to hot pennies being thrown to the crowds - an apparently philanthropic gesture which seemed to amuse the gentry as the children burnt their fingers. But very quickly the peasants learned to come to the fair wearing gloves.

The Hot Pennies ceremony still takes place every year in the High Street at the start of the carnival week. At noon, the Town Crier, accompanied by the Mayor and other local dignitaries, raises a garlanded pole with a gloved hand at the top, and proclaims that, "The glove is up. No man may be arrested until the glove is taken down". Pennies - warmed rather than hot these days - are then thrown from the balcony of the Assembly Rooms above the Old Pannier Market, and a procession follows the garlanded pole to a number of pubs where 'hot pennies' are thrown to the children. The event has been going on annually for hundreds of years. I really like these old traditions.

December

Honiton to Exeter and Exmouth

Pereunt et imputantur,
'The hours pass and are reckoned to our account'
(Exeter Cathedral Astronomical Clock)

Little Egret

Charismatic Animals Return

A short diversion from the main road to Exeter takes us into Ottery St. Mary, straddling the River Otter that runs south to flow into the English Channel at Budleigh Salterton. The name of the river comes from the animals that were common here before numbers were devastated by the cruel so-called sport of otter hunting with dogs. Then in the 1950s farmers began to use organochlorine pesticides that washed into rivers and worked their way up the food chain. These either killed the otters or affected their breeding. Water pollution from herbicides, fertilizers, farm slurry, industrial effluent and sewage also added to the problem. In 1978 the otter had become so rare in England that it was given legal protection and in 1981 the practice of otter hunting with specially bred dogs called otter hounds was outlawed. Chlorine-based pesticides have also been banned.

This protection, along with intervention by wildlife groups that created otter holts along the rivers, has had the desired affect, and these beautiful but elusive animals are now back all along the river that bears their name. In recent years they have been joined by another aquatic animal that was made extinct by human activity. In 2014, wild beavers of unknown origin were found to have bred successfully in the Otter Valley. The government initially planned to have them removed, fearful that they might cause damage, but the Devon Wildlife Trust proposed a different plan. They consulted farmers and landowners before launching the 'River Otter Beaver Trial' in 2015, with pairs of beavers released into likely areas and their activities closely monitored. It became clear that their lodges were beneficial in regulating the flow of the river. Now there are at least fifteen family groups of beavers living throughout the length of the River Otter and some of its tributaries.

A good spot to see them is around Otterton with its ancient watermill still producing flour while offering teas by the river and a range of local food products and arts and crafts. The volunteer serving me in the shop there said, "I've never seen a beaver. Actually, I've never seen an otter either, and I've lived here all my life." Both these aquatic mammals are pretty nocturnal and shy, so I'm not really surprised, but the Devon Wildlife Trust is now organising Beaver Walks on summer evenings - closely supervised of course - and you have to book in advance to get the chance of seeing these fascinating animals. And now a commercial company is organising 'Beaver and Wildlife Tours in East Devon'. Wildlife tourism has become very important for the local economy.

Ottery

Ottery St. Mary, called by the locals simply 'Ottery', is named after the impressive parish church known as the 'Mini Exeter Cathedral' because it was built on similar lines with two towers over the transepts. Like the cathedral it has a 14th century astronomical clock, one of the oldest in the country that is still working, with Earth at the centre of the solar system, orbited by the golden sun and the black and white moon. Ottery was the birthplace of Samuel Taylor Coleridge, and dare I mention that Harry Potter fans may recognise it as Ottery St. Catchpole, the home town of the Weasley family. The riverside walk will take you past a rare 'tumbling weir'. It's like a large plug hole in the bed of a man-made drainage channel that funnels the water through a culvert into the River Otter. But the town's main claim to fame comes from two annual events, one child-friendly, the other terrifying.

Pixie Day

According to local legend, Ottery St Mary was once occupied by Pixies. They were forced into exile by the coming of the humans and the building of the church. The last straw was the noise of the church bells which the little folk couldn't bear, and they believed that each time the bells were rung a Pixie would die. So on midsummer's day in 1454 they crept into town, captured all the bell ringers and imprisoned them in a cave by the river. This cave is still known as Pixies' Parlour. Fortunately for the town, the bell ringers escaped, but the capturing of the bell ringers by the Pixies is re-enacted each year with events on the Saturday nearest to midsummer.

Children from the Guides and Scouts groups, the Brownies, Beavers, Cubs and Rainbows, dress up and play the part of the Pixies in 'The Revenge'. They return to the church and hide, waiting to jump out and capture the bell ringers. Once captured, the bell ringers are imprisoned, but every year they manage to escape. Then there are celebrations with a fete of stalls and entertainment at the Land of Canaan recreation area. In the early evening, 'The Pixies' Revenge' is performed in the square and then the celebrations continue with entertainments, barbecue and bar. I find these old stories of pixies and fairies fascinating. To this day these legends are strong in the old Celtic areas of northern Europe, among them the Cornish Piskies, Leprechauns in Ireland, Scottish Faeries, and the 'Hidden People' in Iceland. They all share the same characteristics – they are small, resentful of being displaced, have magic powers, are mischief-makers, and are closely connected to the natural world that humans don't respect. Shakespeare drew the woodland sprites in 'A Midsummer Night's Dream' from these old legends that are still quite widely believed in some country areas.

Flaming Barrels

From midsummer to the darkness of Bonfire Night, and the other annual event that draws crowds to Ottery. There's a massive bonfire and a fairground, but the main feature on November 5th is the running of the flaming tar barrels. Friends of ours who live in the area invited my wife and me to join them for Bonfire Night in Ottery. We didn't expect it to be quite such a bonkers event. Thousands cram into the centre of town. We were warned not to get trapped among the tightly packed crowds in and around the main street, so we managed to find a vantage point in a raised churchyard overlooking the scene. Even there behind railings, it was scary.

The barrels have been soaked in tar for a week, so they burn fiercely. Burly blokes, and a few strong women, hoist the burning barrels on their shoulders, and run through the chanting crowds. There are seventeen barrels, some as heavy as thirty kilos. The scene is enveloped in acrid smoke, and as the flaming barrels pass, there's a blast of heat. How the carriers manage it is beyond me. Why they do it is also beyond me. No one seems quite sure. Apparently the running of the flaming tar barrels began in the 17th century, but it could have been an older tradition. It may have been the revival of a pagan ritual designed to cleanse the streets of evil spirits. Whatever the reason for this ritual, the surging crowds under clouds of black smoke, lit from below by orange spurts of fire as the flaming barrels are run through, is something once experienced, never forgotten.

Exeter

The A30 takes us across the M5 into the centre of Exeter, the county town of Devon. It is the southwest terminus of the Fosse Way where in AD 55, after suppressing the Dumnonii tribe of the Ancient Britons who ruled modern Devon and Cornwall, the Romans established a large rectangular fort covering 42 acres. It was the base of the 5,000-man Second Augustan Legion commanded by Vespasian, later to become Emperor in Rome. They called the settlement on the River Exe, *Isca*, meaning water-town or river-town. Twenty years later the legion was moved to Caerleon in South Wales to strengthen their operations against the troublesome Welsh. Being on the banks of the River Usk, it was also called *Isca*, so to distinguish the two, the Romans also referred to Exeter as *Isca Dumnoniorum*, 'Watertown of the Dumnonii Tribe', and Caerleon as *Isca Augusta*.

After the withdrawal of the Roman legions, it was the turn of the invading Saxons to drive away the Britons and reinforce the Roman walls, many of which can still be seen today. Exeter was known to the Saxons as *Escanceaster*. In 876 it was briefly captured by Danish Vikings, but Alfred the Great drove them out the following year and further reinforced the city walls. The next invaders from mainland Europe, the Normans, also had to fight for possession of this important city. Two years after the Norman conquest, Exeter rebelled against King William. The mother of King Harold, who had been slain at Hastings, apparently with an arrow in his eye, was living in Exeter at the time. William promptly marched his army west and laid siege to the walled city. After 18 days, the city surrendered, with the conqueror swearing an oath not to harm the city. But he quickly arranged for the building of Rougemont Castle, now known as Exeter Castle, in a corner of the walled city, and garrisoned it to guarantee Norman control of the area.

The Cathedral

Just to the south of the castle, at the centre of the original Roman settlement, stands one of Europe's finest medieval cathedrals, in a wide grassy cathedral close. Construction of Exeter Cathedral began in 1112, but it took another 88 years before it could be declared complete. Much of the Norman stonework and decorations survive, including the detailed carvings of saints and Biblical scenes on the West Front, the soaring nave with the longest medieval stone vaulting in the world, and beautiful 14th century glass in the Great East Window.

There's some extraordinary early wood-carving in the cathedral, including a complete set of fifty misericords under the tip-up seats in the choir, dating from the 13th century. One shows an elephant. Surely no one in Devon had seen one. Historians reckon it was copied from a drawing of the elephant sent to Henry III by Louis IX of France in 1255. And if you visit, don't miss the unique minstrels' gallery in the nave with twelve carved and painted angels playing medieval instruments including a cittern, bagpipe, hautboy, and a crwth, (an early violin from Wales). The most striking piece of wood-carving is the Bishop's Throne in the choir, carved from Devon oak, with its ornate cover over the throne itself towering 60 feet to the roof.

Fortunately the throne was removed just before WWII, along with all the glass from the East Window, the misericords, and the ancient documents of Edward the Confessor and King Athelstan, in case of attack by German bombers. It turned out to be a wise precaution. On May 4th 1942, an early morning raid took place over Exeter as part of the 'Baedeker Blitz' on cultural centres. The cathedral took a direct hit from a high explosive bomb. The Chapel of St. James was demolished along with two flying buttresses and the medieval wooden screen. All have been carefully repaired and reconstructed.

The Hours Pass...

In the north transept stands a large astronomical clock dating from about 1484, though restored several times since. It still chimes every quarter, and the hours are struck by the 'Peter Bell' in the tower above. The Latin inscription under the main dial, *Pereunt et imputantur*, is translated as, 'The hours pass and are reckoned to our account'. So use your time wisely. There's a round hole at the bottom of the clock's wooden casing in a door that leads to the clock room housing the mechanism. They say the hole was cut to allow the cathedral cat to keep the clock works clear of mice and rats, and some say the Exeter timepiece was the inspiration for the old nursery rhyme, Hickory Dickory Dock.

Visitors frequently pass some pleasant time sitting on the low wall around the cathedral close to eat their sandwiches and admire the soaring architecture. This suits the pigeons that wander about picking up crumbs from beneath your feet, but rather less welcome are the herring gulls that lurk on the grass hoping to grab a meal.

A Gull Cull?

These big gulls stir strong feelings in coastal towns, some residents regarding them as a menace that should be controlled through culling. The Daily Mirror called them 'Public Enemy Number One' in a special article describing how they have attacked small pets and caused head-wounds on people wandering too close to their fledglings.

Away from population centres, gulls are omnivorous, eating carrion, worms, fish and shellfish, fruit, young or sick birds, and small mammals. One has even been filmed killing and swallowing a squirrel! Gulls have gizzards that extract the nutrition from their prey, and the bones and skin are coughed up as a pellet. In seaside resorts they have certainly become bold opportunists with a taste for chips, sandwiches and ice cream cones. On a beach near Exeter, my daughter-in-law had a beef sandwich neatly taken from her hand in a surprise aerial manoeuvre by a herring gull. It gave her a nasty shock. But like most wild birds, gulls are protected by law. It is illegal to kill them or interfere with their nests. In fact the herring gull is on the RSPB red list of endangered species because of declining numbers. The regular 'Seabirds Count' conducted by the Joint Nature Conservation Committee found that there were about 51,000 pairs of herring gulls nesting at natural sites rather than in towns and cities, a fall of 41% in the twenty years to 2021. Nearly four times as many were nesting in urban locations, mainly seaside towns. Daisy Burnell, the committee's senior marine biologist, said, "We can't exclude the possibility that some of the gull population has moved into the urban habitat where there are more safe nest sites and good food availability."

A few years ago, a YouGov poll suggested that a small majority of people support the idea of a gull cull, and the great gulls debate reached Westminster with an adjournment debate called 'Seagulls in Coastal Towns'. Some MPs aired the concerns of their constituents about these 'aerial terrorists', but other speakers were strongly opposed to a mass killing of protected birds, and nothing has changed. I think we have to learn to live with gulls, never feeding them or leaving out food waste, keeping your sandwiches in a box on the beach, and being on your guard with your fish and chips or that 99-cone. And there are plenty of ways to deter them from nesting on your flat roof; a network of wires is the most effective way of keeping them away. After all, the seabirds were here before we were.

The cathedral in Exeter is unusual in that it doesn't have a nesting pair of peregrines in residence, which probably accounts for the number of pigeons pecking about on the green. The reason is that the territory belongs to a pair that have nested for more than 20 years in the tall tower of the nearby Church of St. Michael and All Angels. So the pigeons must keep a wary eye out when they fly away from the protection of people. And there are certainly large crowds in the centre of the city at this time of year.

Christmas in Exeter

In December, Exeter is all lit up for Christmas. From mid-November the Cathedral Green is covered in stalls and awnings for the 'Exeter Cathedral Christmas Market', which draws people to the city from around the south-west. The winding lanes between the stalls and chalets are festooned with coloured lights, and there are inviting smells of bacon rolls and mulled wine. A short stroll from Cathedral Close takes us to the main shopping area of Exeter, with a pedestrianised High Street, (except for buses), draped with golden lights. The 'Guildhall Shopping and Dining' covered area, and the 'Princesshay' precinct that was built in the 1950s after the WWII Baedeker raid had demolished much of the city centre, offer all the main retail chains and food outlets - like a cathedral to mammon maybe? The shopping zone in Exeter is pretty compact lying inside the old Roman walls, with a few medieval buildings that survived the blitz in narrow streets near the River Exe.

Among them in West Street is one that has an interesting past. Built around 1450, the Tudor House is half-timbered, with three stories that are 'jettied' meaning that each floor projects further than the floor below in order to get maximum living space for the plot. It's called 'The House That Moved' because until 1961 it was on the corner of Edmund Street and Frog Street 80 yards away. Exeter City Council was planning a ring road and a new road bridge across the river to keep the traffic out of the town centre. Edmund Street and Frog Street were on the route and scheduled for total demolition. 'Wait a moment', said local heritage groups. 'You can't demolish The Tudor House!' So after a lot of debate and sourcing of heritage grants, it was agreed that the house could be moved. It was an extraordinary operation to strip it down to its frame, jack it up on to metal wheels on rails, turn it through 90 degrees, then move it inch by inch up an incline to its new home. Being top-heavy, it was particularly perilous for the Tudor House. But it made it to its new home and is now an attraction.

Horrid Weather

The Christmas shoppers seem to have been undeterred by lots of rain. The weather has been awful for the first half of December, with floods across much of the country. The fields in The Midlands and West Country are saturated, with small groups of sheep huddled on islands of higher ground surrounded by water. More than 1,000 homes have been flooded according to the Environment Agency, and at Christmas time there are more than 300 flood warnings in place in central England. Approaching the Winter Solstice, the succession of Atlantic fronts has passed through, leaving clearer skies for a few days. The trees are skeletons, silhouetted against the low winter sun that struggles to rise above the tree-line at midday, apart from a few oaks that seem to hold on to their brown leaves longer. It's cold, but there's no sign of snow. Then the storms return. There have been seven named storms in the month, with widespread flooding across the West Country and Midlands – the sixth wettest December on record for central England. And it has become milder; in fact it's the sixth warmest Christmas Day on record. This kind of winter weather has become a familiar pattern. White Christmases seem to be a thing of the distant past.

Dreaming of a White Christmas

According to the Met Office, based on the east side of Exeter, Christmas in the UK is designated as white if just one snowflake is observed falling somewhere on December 25th. But their observation stations also report snow on the ground, which is what we all mean by a white Christmas. The Met Office spokesperson, Nicola Maxey, says, "For widespread and substantial snow on the ground on Christmas Day, we have to go back to 2010. In the sixty years to 2020, London had six white Christmases, Edinburgh and Belfast each had eleven, and Cardiff had just four. Climate change has brought higher average temperatures over land and sea and this generally reduces the chances of a white Christmas." It seems Bing Crosby's nostalgic dream is becoming ever more remote. But around the time he was crooning in the early 1940s, a frosty yuletide wasn't so unusual. The winter of 1939-40 was one of the coldest on record.

The winters of 1946-47 and 1962-63 were also notable for heavy snow. And when Dickens was publishing 'A Christmas Carol' in 1843, it followed a cluster of really cold Christmases. As our climate warms, the prospect of an old-fashioned snowy Christmas becomes more and more flakey. And we might recall that Christmas Day has moved! In 1752, The Julian Calendar was replaced by the Gregorian Calendar, changing the formula for calculating leap years. The beginning of the legal new year was moved from March 25th to January 1st. And 11 days were removed from the month of September. So December 25th was in effect brought forward to earlier in the winter. Snow is now more likely in January, February or March.

The Exe Estuary

The Romans who built the Fosse Way also paved the routes from Exeter to the harbours where supplies could be brought in from northern France and Holland. Topsham, three miles south of the centre of Exeter, lies on the east bank of the River Exe where it flows into the long estuary. The sheltered site was a bustling port in Roman times and continued for centuries as a maritime hub, with shipbuilding and long-distance trading as far as Newfoundland. Now it is a picturesque sailing and fishing centre with quaint cottages, handsome houses, narrow alleys, and a host of welcoming pubs and restaurants. I can recommend the dressed crab sold in a fresh fish deli at the Salutation Inn in Fore Street, and the scallops dish served in their restaurant. There is a council-run ferry across the River and a commercial ferry service to the Turf Hotel and Pub on the west bank, which also has birdwatching tours around the estuary at this time of year.

But you don't have to take a boat to see some fabulous bird life here. A short walk from Topsham Quay takes you to the RSPB reserve of Bowling Green Marsh, one of the best places along the south coast to see birds in winter time. It's the main high tide roost for the estuary, so from a well-placed hide, you can see large numbers of waterbirds at very close range. Easy to spot at the water's edge there are nearly always a few pure white little egrets. Hundreds of black-tailed godwits with their long bills often feed quite close to the hide, along with the colourful wigeon. Throughout the year, the open water attracts many different species of wetland birds. There are little grebes, plenty of mute swans, diving ducks such as pochard and tufted ducks, and several hundred avocets are an amazing sight, considering they were extremely rare in Britain just fifty years ago. They sweep the mud with their unusual upward-turned bills, collecting small shrimps and worms.

Reflections

Green and Pleasant Land

Everything is fruit to me that your seasons bring, Nature.
All things come of you, have their being in you, and return to you.
(Marcus Aurelius)

Grey Heron

Human Behaviour

The Fosse Way cuts a line through England revealing our past. But do we learn from history? The Roman Empire was one of the most influential in our turbulent history. Its language, culture, law, art and architecture, influence billions of people to this day. At its height, it ruled almost the whole of Europe, North Africa and Western Asia. In England, while Hadrian's Wall marks the north-western reach of this huge empire, the Fosse still serves as a kind of boundary between the comfortable south-east and the grittier north-west of England. But we should reflect that the empire was based on military might, dominating invaded countries through massacres, slavery and plunder. And over the following two thousand years after the Roman Empire had collapsed, our islands were invaded time and again, soaking the green and pleasant land with blood, as powerful and privileged men sought power and wealth.

In modern times has very much changed? We now face new challenges, but many of the threats are similarly motivated. There are terrible wars inspired by territorial dominance and tribalism. Even climate change is caused by human activity. Conflicts and global heating are leading to mass migration by millions of people seeking peace, security, prosperity and justice. It is easy to become depressed, with many young people in particular feeling disheartened and anxious. It is hardly surprising when we have triple crises affecting our living environment: a 'Climate Crisis', a 'Biodiversity Crisis' and a 'Pollution Crisis'. They are closely linked.

Biodiversity

The latest edition of Britain's 'State of Nature' report, based on the work of 60 research and conservation organisations, made for difficult reading. It lays bare the stark fact that nature is still seriously declining across the UK, a country that is already one of the most nature-depleted in the world. Since 1970 when monitoring began, UK species have declined by about 19% on average, and loss of diversity is continuing. Nearly half of our bird species declined in numbers since 2015. If the trend continues, nearly 1 in 6 species (16.1%) are threatened with extinction. Only a fifth of farmland is in nature-friendly schemes; less than half of our woodland is sustainably managed. Particularly concerning is the reduction in flying insects, a 60% fall according to scientists at the Natural History Museum. These are essential pollinators, and birds that depend on them such as swallows, swifts and martins, are inevitably fewer in number.

Climate Change

In 2007 I was at an international conference hearing about the latest report from the Intergovernmental Panel on Climate Change (IPCC) with data from top climate scientists around the world. They had concluded that the release of greenhouse gases caused by human activity such as power generation, transport and intensive farming, was the main driver of global heating and predicted more extreme weather events such as storms and floods, expanding deserts, rising sea levels as ice melts, and intolerably hot summers in some countries. Every one of those predictions has come true and since then nearly every year has been hotter than the last with the trend accelerating. In Britain we have had more Atlantic storms, serious flooding, and summer droughts. Governments have been painfully slow to take the necessary steps to reduce our emissions and protect communities from the inevitable consequences, such as annual flooding. It's a complicated and expensive challenge that the relatively short political cycle is ill-fitted to grasp.

Pollution

And if that wasn't enough to contend with, we are continuing to pollute our living environment. The dire state of our water and waste infrastructure hit the headlines as it became clear that the privatised water companies were pumping obscene amounts of raw sewage into our rivers and seasides. Air pollution in our cities is now known to affect young children in particular, with more cases of asthma and underdeveloped lung capacity. The benefits of electric vehicles continue to be hotly debated. How is the electricity they use generated? How much carbon is emitted in the manufacture of batteries with mining for lithium and cobalt despoiling large areas of land. And what about the emissions from transporting vehicles across the world, mainly from China at present? But one thing is certain – they are reducing air pollution on our roads.

What can we do?

It is easy to feel helpless in the face of hostile forces abroad and environmental challenges at home, not to mention the financial worries that affect so many people. But I think there is plenty we can do as communities and as individuals, and there are reasons to be optimistic. Marcus Aurelius in his 'Mediations' emphasised that the natural world which sustains human life should be our model and comfort. Regular contact with nature is known to be very beneficial for our physical and mental health. We live in a beautiful land. We should all resolve to regularly take time out in woods, parks or nature reserves, particularly families with children who need fresh air but also want to satisfy a natural curiosity about wild creatures.

And we should all support the charities and trusts that are doing so much to protect and restore wild Britain.

The combined membership of the Wildlife Trusts, the RSPB, National Trust, Woodland Trust, Canal and River Trust, and many other environmental organisations runs into many millions. And it is absolutely clear that just as human activity has damaged our environment over the centuries, human intervention is now having a positive impact. The Wildlife Trusts now care for 2,300 reserves with 39,000 volunteers doing great work to restore habitats that sustain threatened species. The RSPB has more than 200 large reserves, many restoring valuable wetlands and making them accessible to millions of visitors. Specific projects to return to our countryside extinct or rare species, such as the red kite, cranes, beavers, otters, dormice, the large blue butterfly, and many more diminished species, are a success. If you are fit enough to get stuck in as a volunteer with habitat management, don't hold back!

Modern Farming

Farmland accounts for around 69% of land use in the UK. Environment scientists all agree that intensive agriculture has been the primary reason for habitat loss and biodiversity decline. Farming is a very hard business, and there is constant pressure on farmers to produce more of our home-grown food. But this cannot be at the expense of our wildlife. Dumping slurry into our rivers, using pesticides that also finish up in our watercourses, or clearing old woodland and hedgerows to make pasture or arable land is, to my mind, unacceptable. But change is afoot. The former Head of Agriculture at the Morton Morrell College, Jack McDill, now an advisor on sustainable faming, says, "There is definitely a changing mindset among many farmers. Modern farming methods can dramatically reduce the use of pesticides and fertilisers. New methods of soil management are growing, including less ploughing, and more farms are making sure there are untouched fringes to the fields and more wildlife corridors."

He says this needs education, and a holistic approach. 'Natural England', (the government's advisory body for the natural environment with a mission to protect and restore our natural world), already works with farming organisations to help stop biodiversity decline. The Nature Recovery Network is a plan by Defra and Natural England to bring together partners, policies and funding to strengthen and grow nature recovery in England. They say this will help to restore, enhance and connect the natural environment to create more wildlife-rich places, as identified in the 2010 review of England's wildlife sites, 'Making Space for Nature'. I believe Natural England should go even further and create a special body involving farmers, retail chains, conservationists, the Environment Agency, and agri-scientists, with the body having some say about allocation of grants, and the powers to help it push ahead with a new model of farming that is fully sustainable and non-polluting.

There are increasing numbers of projects at local level seeking to achieve this collaborative approach. Here's one example. For several years The Wildlife Trusts have worked with the Jordans Cereals company in the 'Jordan Farms Partnership'. The 30 farms that provide oats for this business are committed to allocating 10% of their land for wildlife. They say there are observable improvements in the numbers of pollinating insects, wildflowers and birds in the re-wilded areas. And the businesses are doing well.

Action

As consumers we can express our opinions through social media, but also in the supermarket. Jack McDill says we can look for the 'LEAF' logo linking wildlife and farming. It's appearing on a growing number of food items and he says it's much more meaningful than the old red tractor symbol. And if we think we can afford the small price premium, we should buy locally sourced organic produce when we can, to encourage this expanding sector. We can lobby our local councils to manage their public land with wildlife in mind. Parks are not just for swings and football fields. And if we are fortunate enough to have a garden, we should make sure we retain some wild areas. Gardens and parks have become hugely important for many species of insects, amphibians, small mammals and birds.

But apart from joining environmental charities that have some leverage on Government policy, we can use our votes wisely at election times. Achieving 'Net Zero' on greenhouse gas emissions is an important target. Some political parties seem to have little interest in restoring our natural heritage, continuing to support fossil-fuel generation. Voters can choose to reject those who promote production and profit over the impact on the wild world. Analysis shows clearly that young people value environmental protection extremely highly. And, of course, they are the future.

I feel confident that those in the growing movement that wishes to stop biodiversity decline, pollution of our rivers, and climate disruption, will make their voices heard loudly in the coming years. It is encouraging that a GCSE in Natural History is being developed as I write - about time! It will be a popular choice, and knowledge about the natural world will be essential if the next generations are motivated to protect it. A year on the Fosse, observing wildlife along the way, reminded me that we have a wonderful natural heritage. Despite the obstacles, we must act, as best we can, to protect it.

The rational person is able to finesse every obstacle and opposition into an opportunity, and to use it for whatever purpose it may suit. (Marcus Aurelius, Roman Emperor and Stoic Philosopher)

The Author

Rick Thompson is a former journalist and broadcaster and a lifelong birdwatcher. He worked for BBC News for 27 years, starting at BBC Birmingham where he produced and presented regional wildlife programmes as well as reporting the news. He moved to London where he became a senior editor with BBC Television News and The World Service. Later he returned to the Midlands as the BBC's Head of News, Current Affairs and Local Programmes. Since leaving the BBC, his consultancy, 'T-Media', has organised dozens of training workshops and development projects across the former Communist countries of Europe, helping to promote independent, high-quality broadcast journalism.

For several years Rick wrote and illustrated a regular column on birds for the Countryside magazine, and for four years he was a member of the Governing Council of the RSPB. He has been asked to moderate many European conferences on the environment, sustainable energy, biodiversity and climate change.

He says, "The great Fosse Way, built and paved with stone soon after the Roman invasion of Britain in AD 43, runs for 230 miles straight through the centre of England. Many of our present day towns and cities were founded beside Roman forts at river-crossings along the route. To pave the road, the invaders quarried stone from the limestone ridge that follows a similar line, and more than two thousand years later, some of these quarry sites are beautiful nature reserves within easy reach of urban centres.

I believe that exposure to nature is incredibly important for people's physical and mental well-being, and getting to know more about the natural world is fascinating. A visit to a bird reserve is particularly uplifting, as well as being good exercise. I hope this month-by-month account of a journey from Lincolnshire to Devon through the heart of England will encourage the reader to get out into the natural environment, and enjoy the variety of wildlife as the seasons change. I also hope you enjoy the stories of the towns and cities along the Roman road, their folklore and legends, and the key moments in England's history that have been played out along the ancient route. The Fosse Way has many tales to tell."

Other books by this author.

'Park Life' – A Year in the Wildlife of an Urban Park.
Grosvenor House Publishing

'A River Avon Year' – The Wildlife and History
of Shakespeare's Avon. Grosvenor House Publishing

'Writing for Broadcast Journalists'.
Routledge